NIKA HAZELTON

The Art
of Cheese Cookery

**MORE THAN 250 RECIPES—
TESTED BY FLORENCE ARFMANN**

PAN
P.O. Box 4416
Berkeley, Calif.
94704

Library of Congress Cataloging in Publication Data

Hazelton, Nika Standen
The art of cheese cookery.

Includes index.
1. Cookery (Cheese) I. Title.
TX759.H38 1977 641.6'7'3 77-2309
ISBN 0-89496-004-0 lib. bdg.
ISBN 0-89496-003-2 pbk.

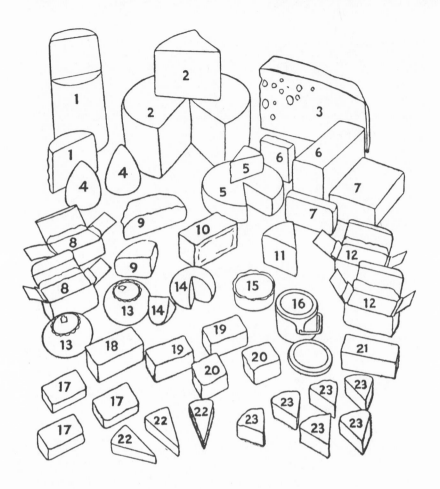

1. American (longhorn style)	12. Limburger
2. American (flat style)	13. Gouda
3. Swiss	14. Edam
4. Pineapple	15. Brie
5. Asiago	16. Natural Packed Cheese
6. American (10-lb. print)	17. Cream
7. Brick	18. Pasteurized Process American
8. Limburger	19. Primost
9. Monterey Jack	20. Cottage
10. Limburger	21. Gjetost
11. Gorgonzola	22. Blue Sectors
	23. Camembert

Courtesy of the National Dairy Council

For Frances Phillips

Acknowledgments

I would like to thank all the people who have given me their help so unstintingly, especially Florence Arfmann.

My thanks go to Dr. G. Saunders of the United States Department of Agriculture, to the National Dairy Council, to the National Cheese Institute, to Messrs. W. Shanks and O. Link of the Kraft Foods Company, to Miss Rachel Reed of the Borden Company, to Mr. L. Weil of June Dairy Products Company, to Mr. K. M. Royer of the Purity Cheese Company, and to Mr. F. J. Klensch of Tolibia Cheese Corporation.

I am much indebted to Mr. A. Dolder of the Switzerland Cheese Association and to Mr. G. Kubly of Monroe, Wisconsin.

I could never have written this book without the most generous technical advice of Dr. L. K. Riggs of the National Dairy Company, of Professor W. V. Price of the University of Wisconsin, and Mr. A. Gruning of Tolibia Cheese Company. My deep thanks for their patience and understanding.

Finally, I want to thank all the friends who have contributed recipes, especially Charlotte Montgomery, Lois Gilbert, and Henriette Seklemian.

Contents

THE ART OF CHEESE COOKERY

What Is Cheese?

CHEESE is a natural miracle. It is nothing short of amazing that a highly perishable fluid such as milk can be transformed into a long-keeping, good-to-eat solid food like cheese.

Cheese is one of the oldest foods known to humanity, so incredibly old that its origins are shrouded in legend, so universal that it appears wherever man has grazed animals and used their milk.

The reason that cheese can be made at all is that under certain circumstances milk will thicken and separate into two different substances. The liquid one is whey and the other, soft, semisolid one is curd. Cheese is the curd of milk, and it can be eaten as is, as Little Miss Muffet did when she ate her curds and whey. Or it can be treated, and ripened into a surprising number of varieties. As with any new food, people first ate cheese because they liked the taste. Then they found it agreed with them, and that it sustained them in the way a proper food does, making them fit for hard work. They included cheese more and more in their diet, until it became a regular staple food with certain peoples.

The Swiss, for instance, eat more cheese than any other nation, and they are a strong, good-looking, and hard-working people. So are the Dutch and Danes, who come next in cheese eating. The people in the cheese business in Wisconsin and other cheese centers who are cheese lovers as well as cheese dealers, are no pikers themselves when it comes to looks and endurance. But in general we Americans rank fairly low in cheese consumption.

CHEESE IS NOURISHING   It isn't surprising that people should thrive on cheese. Like the milk it's made from, it is a nearly perfect food, with a great many of the essential food elements the human body needs. Cheese, of course, has them in a concentrated form. In a pound of American Cheddar cheese you get the equivalent of the milk fat contained in 4 quarts of milk and the protein that is in 2⅖ quarts of milk. Besides, the butterfat in cheese is a good source of vitamin A, which helps the body to resist colds and promote growth. Cheese contains other necessary vitamins, too, but to a lesser extent.

Cheese is a food rich in the muscle- and bone-building foodstuffs. It's full of proteins for body building and has calcium and phosphorus for sound bones and teeth. It's fine for children to grow on, and in a very pleasant way it helps adults to keep their health.

Of course some cheeses are more nourishing than others, depending on whether they're made from whole or skimmed milk and the way in which they are worked. But all cheese is wholesome and nutritious food, and one of the best substitutes for meat.

Many tables have been drawn up by dieticians to show the relative value of one pound of cheese to a pound of this or that cut of meat. To put it simply, you can count on a half pound of Cheddar to provide as much protein as a pound of meat with a moderate amount of bone and fat, and you are perfectly safe building your menus around its food values, or adding it to your diet if you don't have enough other protein foods.

But cheese should not be considered only as a condiment or an occasional snack or as a protein-stretcher. Its high nutritional value makes it eminently suitable for the main dish of any meal. It is the purpose of this book to suggest some of the delicious dishes that can be prepared with cheese. With the usual vegetables, starches, and fruits, a cheese main dish makes a meal that's as well balanced as it is delicious and different.

Cheese is an excellent energy food because it is so concentrated in nourishment. The various varieties differ in caloric content depending on their butterfat. Some cheeses have 435 calories per pound, others as much as 2600. Cottage cheese is at the bottom of the calorie list, with American and Parmesan ranking high. That cheese is nouri.hing is an old story. The Roman writer Pliny tells of Zoroaster, the Persian philosopher, who, a thousand years before Christ, lived for twenty years on nothing but cheese. On a basis of half a pound a day, Zoroaster must have eaten his way through 3650 pounds of cheese!

CHEESE IS DIGESTIBLE One of the old wives' tales was that cheese is hard to digest. This has been disproved by tests made over the years by the United States Department of Agriculture and a large number of scientific institutions. It has been proved, in tests on grownups, that cheese is 90 to 99 per cent digestible. If cheese were really indigestible when eaten often and in large quantities, the leading cheese-eating nations of the world would not have the highest rate of national health, on the basis of longevity and infant mortality rate. After all, cheese is made from milk, and no one would query the healthfulness and digestibility of milk.

In the way of personal experience I would like to report that neither I nor my collaborator has suffered any digestive upsets from eating cheese. Testing all the recipes of this book in the short space of two months, we have eaten our way through I don't know how much cheese of all sorts. We came out of this pleasing experience with an excellent complexion, a fine digestion, and the hearty approval of our families and everybody else on whom we tried our dishes.

But the health-giving properties of cheese are not its only virtues.

Cheese is an economical food. Unlike meat, there is little or no waste. It is inexpensive compared to the nourishment and eating pleasure it gives. It is easy to store. Some varieties keep for a long time.

However, nobody likes a food just because it is nutritionally impeccable. Just as a good woman is much more appealing if she is also attractive and fun to be with, a food has to look appetizing, offer sufficient variety, and taste good.

Cheese certainly is all of these.

CHEESE IS GOOD   There are few cheeses that do not look inviting with their shades of pure white, deep yellow, or prettily veined green-blues. The same appeal is in their shapes, too, and as for the taste, there is no other one food that offers the same enormous varieties of flavors. Cheese is indeed cheese, but there are as many differences between cheeses as there are among human beings. Whatever your fancy turns to—sharp or mild, simple, straightforward, or subtle, there is a cheese that will suit you.

Twenty-five years ago about the only kinds of cheese found in the United States were the common bulk Cheddar and cream and cottage cheese. But now almost all of the cheeses that are famous in Europe are made here also, and are more and more widely distributed in our grocery stores.

As with pudding, the proof of the cheese is in the eating. Without trial and error you'll never find out what you and your family like.

THE HISTORY OF CHEESE Ever since history has been recorded people have eaten cheese. As with all basic foods, its discovery was probably accidental. There are legends of Arab herdsmen who went on a trip, putting their supply of milk in a pouch made from a sheep's stomach. When they opened it, they found curds in the pouch, caused by the heat and shaking of the journey and by the rennet in the sheep's stomach.

As you see, it's a legend. But the fact remains that cheese was known wherever there were milk animals—sheep, goats, water buffaloes, camels, mares, and cows.

At times cheese has been used as money, as South Sea Islanders use shells. Cheese came to Europe from the Near East. The Bible mentions cheese in various places. David was sent with "cheeses" to give to the "captain of their thousand" (I Samuel 17:18).

The Greeks ate and admired cheese and thought it invented by the son of the god Apollo. The diet of athletes training for the Olympics was largely cheese.

The Romans ate lots of cheese and brought it to England, where some of the world's best cheese, Cheddar and Stilton, is still made.

Monks made Roquefort cheese as early as A.D. 1070. Its discovery is another accident: a shepherd lad left his lunch of bread and cheese in the famous Roquefort caves. When he came back, weeks later, he found that the bread had molded and that the cheese looked different. It had a delicious taste, and the shepherd told the monks about it.

Camembert became famous when Napoleon discovered it in an obscure country inn in Normandy. He is said to have been so pleased that he kissed Madame Harel, the maker. In any case, Camembert became the most famous of France's reputed four hundred and fifty cheeses, and Madame Harel had a statue erected to her in her native village.

Italian cheeses, too, are very ancient. Boccaccio, the author of the *Decameron,* writes, in the fourteenth century, of Parmesan on which people lived who had nothing to do except make macaroni and cook them in capon broth.

The Swiss have made Swiss cheese since the sixteenth century. As in all cheese-making countries, curious habits also developed around cheese in Switzerland. There were sections of the country where, at the birth of a child, a wheel of Swiss cheese was made and put away marked with the child's name. For the ceremonial occasions of its life, such as the christening and marriage, slices of its own cheese were cut and served. And at its death and wake the mourners consumed the last pieces in its memory.

Cheese has been made by women as well as by men. It was my privilege to know the best cheese maker, a determined and forceful lady living near Berne, Switzerland. An Englishwoman, Mrs. Masson, who was famous for her Stiltons forty years ago, used to say that "Stiltons, with the exception that they make no noise, are more trouble than babies."

Cheese in America   When the pilgrims sailed on the *Mayflower,* cheese—the round Dutch cheeses—was one of the things they took along.

Until 1850 all the cheese in America was made on the farms. Most of it was cottage cheese, though some farmers also made Cheddar in the way they had made it in their native England.

The first cheese factory was started by Jessie Williams in Oneida County, New York State, in 1851. From then on the number of small plants grew. Until the early nineteen hundreds most of the cheese was made in New York State, where the surroundings were ideal—fine pastures, ample water, a good climate, and wonderful cattle.

By and by the cheese industry traveled westward, especially to Wisconsin, which also had perfect surroundings for cheese making. And today cheese is made in almost every state of the Union.

One of the older American-made cheeses, apart from Cheddar, is Limburger, which was first made by Swiss settlers in Oneida, New York. Now it's made mostly in Wisconsin.

Swiss cheese, too, has been made for a long time. Now most of it is also made in Wisconsin, and Monroe is called the Swiss-cheese capital of the United States. There, the surrounding countryside is picturesque, as the Swiss cheese makers have built themselves Swiss chalets. Especially is this evident in New Glarus.

During the thirties American cheese makers went in for making all the varieties that were no longer coming from Italy. After World War II more and more foreign-type cheeses were made here, proving that we can make any kind of cheese, provided there is enough demand for it.

HOW MANY CHEESES? A great deal of nonsense has been written about cheese by the fancier gastronomes. They represent it as a substance that can't just be eaten plainly and simply, but that has to be celebrated by a high priest and the entire cast of the second act of *Aïda*.

Cheese is not at all an esoteric food, but peasant fare. Lots of very good cheese is still made by people who have never heard of "culinary adventures."

Cheese has been made from any kind of milk—such as mare's, water buffalo's, and camel's. Much of it is made from goat's milk. Roquefort is made from sheep's milk. But most of the cheese made, and almost all of that made in America, is made from cow's milk.

Cheese is known under about four hundred different names. This is a staggering amount, and if you are out to impress people you can dazzle them with Kolos Monostor.

a sheep's milk cheese made in the Agricultural School in Transylvania, or question them on the difference between Brie and Bra cheese.

But four hundred different names for cheese does not mean that there are four hundred different varieties. There are about eighteen basic types of cheese, which crop up under a variety of names both in the same country and in other countries. Italian Gorgonzola, English Stilton, and Danish Blue are all blue-mold cheeses, and Italian Bel Paese is not too different from French Port du Salut.

Cheeses are often named after the locality, country, town, or village from whence they come, such as Roquefort or Cheddar. A cheese with a Serbian name may well have its counterparts in French, Italian, or Czech.

To add to the confusion, different cheese manufacturers sell their own cheeses under a variety of brand names, though they may be very much alike.

But whatever its name, cheese is cheese, and it all is made from milk.

WHAT KIND OF MILK?   The quality of the milk used in cheese making is of the greatest importance—how much can't be stressed enough. The results of the cheese making depend on it. It's staggering for a layman to learn how different milk can be depending on the kind of cows, the pasture, the treatment after milking, and so on. Milk can be rich in fat or poor, gaseous, or have strange flavors if it isn't cooled properly after milking and stored in such a way that it can't pick up any odors.

The cheese makers worry about their milk all the time. They know that even a very small amount of defective milk can ruin a whole batch of cheese. They employ fieldmen who visit the farms advising the farmers on how to get the best milk, though sometimes their advice is not taken in the spirit in which it is given.

Every day, as the milk comes in from the farms, the

cheese plant tests it for purity and for butterfat content. One of the things that makes cheeses different from one another is the quantity of butterfat they contain, though it does not mean that a fatter cheese is better. Cheddar is richer in butterfat than Swiss, but they both are wonderful cheeses.

About the Pasteurization of the Milk and Its Effect on Cheese. After the tests, the milk is usually pasteurized in large vats. Pasteurization makes the milk more wholesome and easier and more reliable to work with, but it changes the flavor of the cheese, making it milder and softer. This is fine for some cheeses, such as cream, cottage, Munster, and the like, but when it comes to cheese that should have a rich, sharp flavor, such as Cheddar, pasteurized milk takes away a great deal of the characteristic tang.

This happens because pasteurization kills all the bacteria, good and bad. The good bacteria have to be put in again later, to give the cheese its taste. Most of the cheese made in America is made from pasteurized milk. It's certainly a good thing for the public, when it comes to perishable cheeses such as cream and cottage. But, on the other hand, it's well to remember that the prolonged curing of cheese kills off harmful bacteria anyway. Europeans and our own forefathers have lived for centuries on cheese made from unpasteurized milk and been none the worse. In many cases they had more highly flavored cheese.

About the Curd After pasteurization, the milk goes into a big vat or kettle, where the "starter" and later the rennet are added to it.

To make cheese, the milk must have a certain degree of acidity. All milk is slightly but varyingly acid, and for cheese making this has to be controlled. With the right amount of acidity, cheese is smooth, silky, and mellow. If there is too much acid, it will be dry, harsh, mealy, or corky. If there is too little acidity, the cheese will have too weak a body and not ripen properly.

In order to get the right amount of acidity, so-called "starter" is added to milk, just as you add vinegar to your milk when you make chocolate cake. Incidentally, the wives of cheese makers make their chocolate cake with "starter" and get a vastly superior cake. There are all kinds of starters, and cheese makers usually make their own.

Rennet is added to the milk to make it curdle. It's like making rennet custard on an enormous and complicated scale.

The Curd Is Cut and Drained   When the milk has curdled, the art of the cheese maker really begins, though he has to know all about his "starter" and the type of rennet he is using, and about their effects.

Depending on the kind of cheese in the making, the curdled milk has to be softer or thicker. The cheese maker can tell if it is by the looks of it, and by patting the curd with his fingers.

When it's right, the curdled milk is cut into curds, which must be even in size. This is done by drawing curd knives through it. These are frames with parallel wires about one-third of an inch apart. The curd is cut horizontally and vertically. If it isn't cut evenly, so that the whey will come out evenly, too, the cheese will be uneven—expelling the whey is the idea behind the curd cutting.

All sorts of tricks come in now. The curds have to be a certain size for the type of cheese that's being made. If they are larger, they retain more whey, and make for a moister cheese. When they are cut again and again, almost to a pinpoint, as for Swiss and Parmesan, they make a harder, drier cheese.

The curd is left to expel the whey for a certain amount of time, the mass of curd and whey being heated to just the right temperature. This is done by circulating steam under and around the milk vats; in the old days on the farm a fire was built under them. The white curd flakes taste like pleasant rubber, and they float in the yellowish whey. The cheese maker watches carefully to get the curd just as firm as he wants it. This sounds simple, but it is a very skillful process, which has to be learned through years and years of practice.

Cheese makers have to know how to make rapid decisions. Milk undergoes chemical changes so quickly that a few seconds' delay may ruin a whole batch of cheese.

After the curd has drained sufficiently, it is put into hoops or molds and pressed into shape. The molds and hoops have holes, so that more whey can be drained off the cheese. Sometimes a cloth is used to keep the curd in shape; this cloth stays on some kinds of cheese right through the rest of the operations, so that when you buy it you will find it still there.

SALTING AND CURING THE CHEESE Cheese, like meat or fish, has to be salted if it is to keep. Sometimes the salting takes place when the curd is still in the whey bath. At other times it is salted when it is out of the hoops or molds, dipping it in a brine bath or rubbing salt on the surface while curing.

The curing or ripening of the cheese is what makes the taste most, because this is the time when the important chemical changes take place.

Cheese can be cured in about as many ways as there are cheeses. It is cured in natural caves, in cellars and storerooms which are kept at the appropriate temperature and degree of moisture.

Cheese is ripened by bacteria and molds. This sounds queer until you remember that there are many *helpful and necessary* bacteria in foods as well as in cheese. The same goes for molds. The molds veining Blue and Roquefort cheeses are of the Penicillium family, from which penicillin is made. And bacteria form the gas that forms the holes in Swiss cheese.

These beneficial bacteria and molds are usually added to

the milk in the first steps of cheese making. Later on, during the ripening process, they really go into action, helped by the conditions in which the cheese is cured and by the length of time.

The science of cheese making consists in controlling the helpful bacteria and molds and excluding the unwanted ones. Cheese makers make their own molds and bacteria in wonderfully modern labs, guarding their cultures with their lives, so to speak, since so much depends on them.

Cheeses ripen in different lengths of time. The longer the time, the sharper the cheese, which is fine with Cheddar and Parmesan. But other cheeses, such as Camembert and Limburger, get much too powerful if ripened beyond the proper time. And cream and cottage cheese must be eaten before they have ripened at all.

The Wrapping of Cheese   When the cheese has ripened for a certain length of time, first in the factory and then in the warehouse, it is graded and wrapped in different ways, to allow further ripening or to stop it.

Some cheeses, such as Cheddar, are dipped in paraffin, which clings close to the rinds. Lampblack is smeared on Parmesan, and Blue and cream cheeses are wrapped closely in tin foil.

To find suitable wrapping materials for cheese is one of the great problems of the cheese industry and one that has not yet been completely solved. The wrapper ought to be transparent, so that you can see what you are buying, and it must have a number of technical qualities to keep the cheese good and yet allow it to ripen properly.

THE BEST-KNOWN VARIETIES   Practically all the cheese we know, make, and eat in America originated in Europe.

Before cheese making became the thoroughly scientific process it is today (with much surer results and fewer failures) there was a reason why certain cheeses came from certain parts of a country.

The soft and humid climate of northern and central France, Belgium, Alsace, and western Germany developed cheeses that are semisoft and ripened from the outside, because of local climatic conditions. Camembert from France and Tilsiter from Germany are examples, and so is Munster from Alsace. They are very different cheeses, but they have a short ripening process in common.

Southern Italy, which is hot, makes hard, long-keeping cheeses such as Romano and the Provolone family, which is smoked to make it keep even better.

Another reason is the supply of available milk. Where there are lots of goats, as in Norway, goat's milk cheese is made; where there are sheep, as in France and Italy, fine ewe's milk cheeses are current.

Since this is not a technical book, but a cookbook, there is no necessity for going into the tricks of cheese making; it also would be exceedingly complicated to explain the exact reasons that make each cheese different.

Cheddar   About 80 per cent of the cheese made in America is American Cheddar, which is what people mean when they call for bulk or store cheese, or just plain cheese.

Cheddar has been made in the English village of Cheddar for centuries, and the early settlers brought their skill for making it when they came to America.

Cheddar is made from whole milk. It is either white or yellow, depending on popular demand. When it is yellow or orange, it has been colored with annatto, a yellow coloring matter made from the seeds of a Central American tree. This is added to the milk before the rennet and does not affect the taste of the cheese or nourishment.

The process which gives Cheddar some of its typical texture is called cheddaring. This is a way of stacking the curd which has been cut into slabs to drain it from the remaining whey. The curd is then put into a milling machine which cuts it into pieces which then go into the hoops.

Cheddar is made in several varieties, such as the "washed curd" and Colby type. It also comes in a half dozen or so shapes, such as daisies, longhorns, et cetera.

Cheddar is not a complicated cheese to make. It is mild, medium, or sharp, depending on the amount of acidity in the milk, the curing, and aging. It is made all over the United States under different brand names. It is called "current" if it is not more than thirty days old, "short held" from one to six months old, and "aged" when more than six months old. The older—up to two years—the richer the tang.

Swiss Cheese   Making Swiss cheese was and is one of the most picturesque occupations of the Swiss mountaineers. It is made in huge copper kettles (nothing but copper will do, anywhere), in which the curd is heated for a long time to expel all the whey and to harden. In the old days huge fires were built under the kettles, but today, both in Switzerland and in the United States the kettles are heated by steam.

The bacteria that gives Swiss cheese its holes, or "eyes," and its sweet nutty flavor, are added to the milk in the beginning.

Swiss cheese is very tricky to make and to cure. More depends on the quality of the milk and the skill of the maker, or the cheese will be a flop; the "eyes" won't be the right shape or size, which is fatal, since the right kind of "eyes" means the right taste, apart from being what Swiss cheese is judged on. Considering that the wheels of Swiss weigh two hundred pounds and more, the losses can be very serious if the cheese goes wrong.

Like Cheddar, Swiss must be aged properly. It shouldn't be eaten before it is three months old. Then its nutty, distinctive flavor makes it another great cheese.

A great deal of Swiss is made in America, especially in

Wisconsin, and much of it is very good indeed, especially when properly aged. But the best Swiss is still made in Switzerland, because the tender, juicy, aromatic grass the cows feed on in the high Alps cannot be duplicated. You recognize Swiss cheese from Switzerland by the word Switzerland all over its rind.

Blue Cheeses Blue cheese, that is, cheese with a greenish-blue network of veins, originated in a number of European countries. In Italy, it's called Gorgonzola; in England, Stilton; in Denmark, Blue; and in France, Roquefort. There are differences in taste in Blue cheese, which their admirers discuss with fervor and passion.

All Blue cheeses are made on the same principle, that is, injecting a mold of the Penicillium family into them to give them veining and piquant flavor. The various Blue cheeses have various Penicillium molds, which account for the variations in flavor. The good cheese makers grow their own molds as jealously and secretly as if they were making gold, which, in a way, they are. The molds are either put into the milk or injected into the cheeses after they have been salted and pierced with many holes. These air holes are needed to give the mold the air it needs to develop.

Blue cheeses are ready to eat after two to three months of ripening. The flavor improves as the cheese gets older. What makes Roquefort into perhaps the best Blue cheese is that it's made from sheep's milk and ripened in the limestone caves of Roquefort in Central France, where the special Penicillium mold grows on the inside. The caves also have a wonderful natural system of ventilation, which keeps the air cool and humid and at the same temperature all the year round. The ripening conditions of Blue cheese are so important that its makers have gone to the greatest trouble to reproduce the atmosphere of the Roquefort caves.

No cheese can call itself Roquefort unless it comes from there and has the name France on the wrapper.

Camembert   It isn't difficult to get the curd of Camembert right, but it's very difficult to cure it properly. The humidity and temperature of the curing rooms must be exactly right. The mold of the Penicillium family that is spread on the un-ripened cheese must be applied just so to make the felty rind that protects the cheese but does not penetrate it.

Then Camembert has to be eaten at the right time, or else it gets too powerful. That is French Camembert, which the French like on the strong side. American Camembert is much milder, and has much less of the characteristic taste, since it's made from pasteurized milk, while the French is not.

Italian-type Cheeses   There is an infinite variety of Italian cheeses which are made in a very different way, so that it is really not fair to lump them under one name.

The best known are the hard grating cheeses such as Parmesan and Romano, the Blue-type Gorgonzola, and the Provoloni.

Parmesan is unquestionably the best grating cheese ever invented by man. It's made very much like Swiss cheese, but from milk that has been partially skimmed. And, like Swiss, Parmesan must have the perfect starter and be heated for a long time to get its dry, granular texture. Then it is cured for a long time, for two years and more. The older the Parmesan, the better the taste.

Romano, in Italy, used to be made from sheep's milk which gave it a pungent flavor. In this country, though, it's made from cow's milk and correspondingly milder. It is hard and granular like Parmesan, and quite a good substitute for it, but nothing can beat Parmesan.

The really curious Italian cheeses are those odd-shaped sausages that hang from the ceiling in Italian neighborhood stories. They belong to the Provolone family, and are made in a strange and complicated way—by pulling the curd in scalding hot water and kneading it by hand. When the cheeses are shaped they are tied up by the complicated system of strings you see on them. The cheese makers wives' do the knotting of the strings. Then they are salted and smoked over a wood fire. When ripened for a period up to six months they make excellent eating. When they are older, the Provoloni are good for grating.

Mozzarella is made in the same way, but it is eaten fresh. Another popular Italian cheese is Ricotta, or Italian-type cottage cheese.

Semihard Cheeses Semihard cheeses are exactly what their name implies. Bel Paese, Munster, Brick, Limburger are good examples, as well as several cheeses of the same type that are marketed under brand names, such as Gold-N-Rich, Elmo, and others.

These cheeses are made and ripened in different ways, but their texture is similar. They are excellent, all-round cheeses for eating and in some cases for cooking. They should be eaten when they are about three months old.

Soft Cheeses The two best-known ones are cream and cottage cheese. They must be eaten soon and be kept under constant refrigeration.

Cream cheese is one of the rare cheeses that profits enormously from pasteurized milk, which makes it even milder. It is made from milk and cream, and in the case of the better-known brands, almost entirely by machine.

Cottage cheese is the simplest cheese to make—milk or skim milk is turned sour and then heated to drain the whey off the curd. Its greatest virtue is that it has a pleasant taste and a low-calorie but high-protein content.

For every one of the cheeses I've been talking about there are a dozen or more that closely resemble them and are as good. You will find the best-known varieties on the Cheese Chart on pp. 41–48. Or a trip to your nearest cheese store will prove to be as much fun as it is instructive.

AMERICAN AND FOREIGN CHEESES   Cheese is now made in almost every state of the Union. But about 50 per cent of all of our cheese is made in Wisconsin.

New York State, as beautifully pastoral as Wisconsin, was a leader in cheese making until the early nineteen hundreds. Then most of the milk it produced was shipped to New York City for drinking purposes.

The cheese industry is different from other industries inasmuch as much cheese is made by small plants, about 3500 in the United States. They sell their cheese to the distributors, who market it under their own brand names. Of course there are big cheese factories, too, owned by Kraft or Borden, and other firms. But the industry is changing in favor of big cheese plants. Their products will be much more uniform, but the individual cheese maker's skill is something no machine can replace. We'll have good cheese that is always the same, but without the individual craftsmen we'll seldom, if ever, have cheese that's outstanding.

Very often American cheese is not sufficiently aged. Aging is expensive, since it involves warehouse space, tender care, and the tying up of large investments. That's why so many manufacturers are reluctant to do it.

One of the reasons why some imported cheeses taste better is not that they are better in themselves, but that they are sufficiently cured. Of course we must also remember that Europe and Argentina send us their choice specimens and eat the run-of-the-mill products themselves.

THE DIFFERENCE BETWEEN NATURAL, PROCESS CHEESE, CHEESE FOOD, AND CHEESE SPREADS This is indeed a controversial subject, and one that's likely to cause a great deal of frank comment.

Natural cheeses are all the cheeses that are made and cured as described in the previous pages, even when they are made from pasteurized milk. Of course they require great care in handling, storing, and marketing, which makes them more expensive and much, much better. There is no substitute for their honest, natural taste.

Process cheese is a blend of various cheeses which is made by heating them together with suitable emulsifiers, so that a uniform plastic mass is achieved. This mass is then packaged mechanically.

The cheese that goes into processed cheese is chosen carefully by professional cheese blenders who select a number of cheeses of different age, to achieve the proper blend for flavor and texture. Most of it is blended for a mild flavor, because that's what many people prefer.

Process cheese is always uniform in whatever degree of sharpness or mildness it has, which is not so with natural cheese. It keeps well and is easy and inexpensive to store. People seem to like its bland flavor and absence of rind— which pleases the manufacturers, who advertise it with abandon and make plenty of money on it.

Cheese food is something else again. It's processed, *and* cream, non-fat milk solids, and mineral salts have been added to it. Some of the calcium and phosphorus that are lost in the whey during cheese making has been restored in cheese food.

Cheese food is certainly nourishing, though it is even milder than process cheese, which makes it immensely mild. It is always made from Cheddar. Like process cheese, it melts easily and smoothly and keeps as well, and it also has no rind.

There are a great many cheese spreads that come in attractive little glasses as well as some that come in sausage and other shapes. Many manufacturers make them by grinding up their products and adding stabilizers and flavorings, such as pimento, bacon, et cetera.

All these subdivisions of process cheese are by law clearly labeled as to their content.

There are tastier and less-tasty kinds of process cheese, just as with natural cheese. Here, too, you have to experiment to find the kind that suits you best.

WHAT CHEESE TO BUY   In America there are cheeses than can be bought throughout the country and others which never leave the locality where they are made.

They are all good, and there is only one thing to do—try them out to see which ones you like best. When you are out buying cheese, look at the labels. The names of companies such as Borden, Kraft, June Dairy, and others are a guarantee as to quality.

Ask your grocer about any local cheeses he might have. Or try cheese specialty stores. Or order cheese by mail. It's fun to get acquainted with new brands, and the man of your house will appreciate it.

I hesitate to give the brand names of the cheeses I like best, because I am positive there are others as good. And each manufacturer makes so many fine brands that it is impossible to mention them all.

With this understanding I shall say that I like Borden Camembert and Kraft Chantelle. I like any sharp Cheddar I am able to find, especially New York State Cheddar. The same goes for aged Swiss. The Gorgonzola and Parmesan of the Stella Company of Wisconsin are excellent, and so are the Gouda and Edam made by the Purity Cheese Company. A very fine eating and cooking cheese is Gold-N-Rich, that is tops for either.

But the cheese that gives me the greatest personal pleasure is Elmo cheese, a semisoft, delicate, and delightful dessert cheese, as fine as any cheese made in Europe. Elmo is made by the Tolibia Cheese Company of Fond du Lac, Wisconsin, which also makes excellent Blue and Italian cheeses.

These are only a few of the wonderful cheeses we make in America. There are scores of others, so sample as many as you can. Good hunting!

HOW TO STORE CHEESE   **Soft, Perishable Cheeses, Such as Cream and Cottage**   Buy only what you need at the time, and treat exactly as you treat your milk and butter. Keep refrigerated, well wrapped, and away from foods with strong odors.

Semihard Cheeses, Such as Brick, Munster, Port du Salut, et cetera These cheeses can be bought in larger quantities, to last you a couple of weeks or so, provided you treat them right. Keep refrigerated, and well wrapped in wax paper, tin foil, plastic food bags, et cetera. Keep at room temperature for one to three hours before serving, to release the flavor, because cheese straight out of the icebox does not have too much taste, being too cold. If mold has formed, simply cut it away — it does not harm the cheese or yourself. On cheeses like Brie and Camembert, the mold adds to the flavor. *And never cut off more cheese than you need at the time.*

Blue Cheeses Apply the rules for semihard cheeses.

Hard Cheeses, Such as Cheddar, Swiss, Parmesan, et cetera You can buy several pounds at a time, if you keep it this way. Buy the cheese in *one* piece, and cut off what you need, to prevent drying out. It is best to refrigerate the cheese, but you can also keep it in a cool place—it must be cool, though. Keep the cheese well wrapped in wax paper or tin foil at all times. If it gets too dry, wrap it in a clean cloth wrung out in vinegar or water. Keep cloth damp.

Process Cheese These cheeses will keep for months in their original, unopened wrapper even without refrigeration. But once you have started using one, rewrap in original wrapper or wax paper *very tightly,* to keep out air. Refrigerate the cheese, and, if possible, place it *wrapped* in food bag or covered refrigerator dish.

Cheese Spreads The unopened jars or glasses will keep for months. Once a jar has been opened, it must be put into the refrigerator, covered, and used up fairly soon, that is within about a week.

refrigerator, covered, and used up fairly soon, that is within about a week.

Grated Cheese Grated cheese ought to be stored in *airtight* containers on the pantry shelf to prevent it from drying out. It is better not to put it into the refrigerator, where it absorbs moisture and lumps easily.

HOW TO PREPARE CHEESE FOR COOKING Soft cheeses ought to be grated on a coarse grater which will give long flakes. Or else they can be sliced thinly into slivers, as in the case of cheese foods.

Hard cheeses, such as Parmasan, et cetera, should be grated on a five grater. Since they dry out quickly, it is best to grate just enough for each use—they also taste better this way.

Cheese should always be cooked at a low temperature if the dish has to cook for any length of time. Else it can be cooked for a very short time at a high temperature. Any other way makes it stringy and tough.

Very dry grated cheese will not melt when heated, unless moisture is added, as in the case of soup.

Cheese that has dried out is still perfectly good and nutritious to use. Make it into macaroni and cheese, souffles, fondues, et cetera, or grate it for soup.

If mold has formed on the cheese, simply cut it off. It won't hurt you or the cheese.

HOW TO SERVE CHEESE The nice thing about cheese is that you can serve it as fancy or plain as you wish and get full enjoyment out of it. It makes an excellent dessert, and it is eaten as such a great deal in Europe and to an increasing extent here in America. If you have a sweet tooth, you will like cream or cottage cheese with preserves or honey or fresh fruit. And among the great variety of cheeses there are bound to be several with which you like to end your meal.

An assortment of cheeses is sure to please your guests at cocktail time, at a buffet luncheon or supper, or for a midnight snack.

You can let yourself really go in arranging a cheese tray. The idea is to have several varieties of cheese for a variety of tastes, and to arrange your cheeses as attractively as you can.

There are many ways of arranging a cheese tray. You can do it around a centerpiece, using a Dutch cheese, with slices of other cheeses around it. Or else you can have it in the Continental manner, wherein the cheeses are placed on the tray in large hunks from which each person cuts off what he wants. The first way is much more decorative and simpler to handle when there is a crowd. The second has the merit that the cheese tastes better, because it has not had a chance to dry out.

It is well to remember that all cheese tastes better, a great deal better, if it is cut into thick, chunky slices rather than thin slices. Instead of having a fairly large thin slice of cheese, try to cut the same quantity into a chunky slice. You'll notice at once the difference in taste.

Do not serve cheese straight out of the refrigerator if you can help it. Let it stand at room temperature for an hour or so to release its full goodness.

It would be impossible to tell you all the ways of arranging a cheese tray. If you run out of ideas, get the booklets and suggestions put out by the cheese companies. They all have excellent recipes and equally attractive ideas on how to arrange a pretty cheese tray.

Be sure to have two or three different kinds of crackers or breads to go with your cheese tray. Some of them go better with certain cheeses than others, and your guests, too, have their preferences.

Have several knives or spread knives on your cheese tray to use on the different cheeses so as not to carry the flavor of one cheese to the other by using the same knife.

To end up with, the simple combination of crisp apples or juicy pears with Roquefort or Blue cheese, or Camembert and Brie (and any other kind you like) is still one of the very best.

HOW TO SUBSTITUTE ONE CHEESE FOR ANOTHER IN COOKING Generally speaking, cheeses can be substituted for one another in cooking. The difference comes in the taste of the dish. A sharp cheese will give a sharper flavor than a mild cheese. Some recipes call for a definite kind of cheese, and that cheese is best for that particular dish. Of course the cheeses substituted for each other must be of the same or similar type. You couldn't substitute Cheddar for Cottage cheese. But if you have Swiss, let us say, instead of Cheddar, you can still make a fine dish—or vice versa.

Parmesan and Romano have a very definite place in cookery, since they are the very best grating cheeses to use on spaghetti, macaroni, rice, and similar dishes. No other cheese, however hard and easy to grate, takes their place. If you don't have any cheese on hand to grate, use the small cartons or envelopes of grated cheese put out by Borden, Kraft, and other companies.

However, since Parmesan and Romano are now so easily bought (if you can't get them at your market, try any grocery store in an Italian neighborhood, or order them from the places mentioned on page 40) and since they are easily stored, I strongly recommend that you have some on hand at all times. Do your own grating (in Italy, grating is the children's job) and you will be rewarded by a flavor that's incomparably better.

As you will see in the recipes of this book, there are many more cheeses to be used in cooking than Cheddar. Swiss is one of them, and it is wonderful with its nutlike flavor. The semihard cheeses, too, are excellent for some dishes, as in fondues, cooked sandwiches, et cetera. There are quite a number of them—the ones that give the best results, in my opinion, are Gold-N-Rich, Mel-O-Pure, and Elmo. However, this does not mean that other cheeses of the kind would not be as good. It just so happens that these are very readily available.

And of course, the process cheeses and cheese foods are good for quick, mildly flavored dishes.

A last hint: to my mind, the best cheese for a delicate soufflé with a definite cheese taste is a mixture of even parts of grated Swiss and Parmesan.

ABOUT THE RECIPES IN THIS BOOK In this book I have tried to give recipes that are not the usual ones. For the old stand-byes you can do no better than to consult your favorite standard cookbook.

A hot oven is 400° to 450° F.
A moderate oven is 325° to 400° F.
A slow oven is 250° to 325° F.

TIPS FOR BUYING CHEESE More and more cheese is sold in consumer sizes. The days when you bought a chunk of cheese from a loaf or a wheel are almost gone. Now, the stores cut up the cheese and wrap it before they put it on the counter, if this has not already been done by the manufacturer.

These consumer-sized packages may have merits for the store, but generally they are thoroughly irritating to the customer, who wants to know what he is buying. There is no way of telling what you are getting, unless you happen to recognize a brand name.

The only way of telling good cheese (I'm not speaking of reliable brand names) from unsatisfactory cheese is to taste it. When the clerk gave you slivers of cheese before buying, you had a chance to judge and decide.

Now, the cheese is all cut up and often dried out, because it is not always properly wrapped, and because a small quantity of cheese dries out much more quickly than a large amount.

Whenever you can, insist on tasting the cheese you have your eyes on. It's worth it every time.

Where to Buy Cheese   Get acquainted with the cheeses in your grocery store. The chain stores particularly carry far more varieties than you thought. Try the fancier markets, and if you live in a sizable town, there is probably a cheese specialty store.

Here are the names of some stores where you can order cheese by mail. This is by no means a comprehensive list of sources. However, these stores carry a large and reliable assortment of cheeses, and they will give you good service.

Macy's Grocery Department, Herald Square, New York, New York.

Stop and Shop Grocery Department, Dearborn Street, Chicago, Illinois.

The City of Paris Grocery Department, San Francisco, California.

For excellent aged Wisconsin Swiss or Cheddar and other types of Wisconsin cheese there is no better source than

The Swiss Colony, Monroe, Wisconsin

They will send you, if you wish, your cheese in very attractive packages that make wonderful presents.

A CHEESE CHART OF THE BEST-KNOWN VARIETIES

Cheese	Origin	Characteristics	Use	How long it may be ripened
American Cheddar	England	Waxed yellow-brown surface. Cream to deep orange inside. Mild flavor when fresh; sharper the more cured and aged	Eating Cooking Processing	One month to two years
Asiago	Italy	Dark surface, creamy inside. Hard granular texture; piquant flavor	Eating when fresh; grating when old and drier	One month to two years
Bel Paese	Italy	Gray-brown surface; light yellow inside. Soft texture, delicate flavor	Eating	Three months
Blue Bleu if imported	France Denmark	Usually foil-wrapped. White interior with blue veins. Semihard. Piquant flavor that gets stronger with age	Eating Cooking	Two months to one year
Brick	United States	Yellowish-brown surface, creamy yellow inside. Semihard and smooth texture. Flavor between Limburger and Cheddar	Eating Processing	Two to nine months

A CHEESE CHART OF THE BEST-KNOWN VARIETIES (*Cont'd*)

Cheese	Origin	Characteristics	Use	How long it may be ripened
Brie	France	Russet-brown surface; creamy yellow inside. Soft, creamy; resembles Camembert. Mild to pronounced flavor. Eat crust	Eating	Four to six weeks
Caciocavallo	Italy	Light brown glossy surface; yellowish inside. Solid body and texture, rather hard. A slightly salty, smoked flavor	Eating Grating when old and dry	Eaten fresh or cured up to one year
Camembert	France	Gray-white mold surface; soft inside. Full flavor, ammoniacal if too ripe. Before serving, store at room temperature until runny. Eat crust	Eating	Four to six weeks
Cottage Cheese	Unknown very old	Soft, white, pleasantly sour flavor. Made from skim milk; some has cream added	Eating Cooking	Not at all

Name	Origin	Description	Use	Ripening
Pot Cheese		A form of cottage cheese with a dry curd. Not creamed		
Cream Cheese	Europe Asia United States	Made from cream and milk. White, delicate, slightly acid taste	Eating	Not at all
Edam	Holland	Red waxed surface; yellowish inside. On the hard side. Mild, Cheddarlike flavor	Eating Cooking	One to three months
Gammelost	Norway	Hard, golden-brown with a strong flavor	Eating	Four to eight months
Gjetost	Norway	Hard; dark-brown with a sweet, uncheeselike flavor. Made from goat's milk	Eating	Four to eight months
Gold-N-Rich Chantelle Mel-O-Pure Elmo	United States (Trade-mark names)	Gold-N-Rich and Chantelle have a red-coated exterior. Mel-O-Pure is yellow. Elmo is lighter. Yellow to golden inside. Semi-soft texture; mild flavor	Eating Cooking	One to three months
Gorgonzola	Italy	Clay-colored surface; white inside, with green veins. Piquant flavor	Eating	Three months to one year

A CHEESE CHART OF THE BEST-KNOWN VARIETIES (*Cont'd*)

Cheese	Origin	Characteristics	Use	How long it may be ripened
Gouda	Holland	Usually red surface. Semi-hard texture, yellow inside. Edamlike flavor if imported. Domestic (Baby) Gouda is softer and has often a slightly sour flavor	Eating	Six to eight months
Gruyère	Switzerland France	Hard, with holes; tastes like Swiss. In United States Gruyère means a process cheese that is foil-wrapped and light yellow	Eating Cooking	Three months to one year; not at all, if processed
Monterey Jack	California United States	Semihard when new; hardens with age. Mild flavor when new	Eating Cooking Grating	Three to four weeks for fresh Jack—more for dry variety
Liederkranz	United States (Trade-mark name)	Russet surface; creamy inside; soft, with robust taste and odor	Eating	Four weeks

Limburger	Belgium	Grayish-brown surface; creamy white inside. When new it's white, tasteless, and without odor. Cured, it is soft, with a full, aromatic taste	Eating	One to three months
Munster	Germany	Yellowish-tan surface. When fresh, white inside; turns yellow with curing. Tastes like Brick, only milder	Eating Cooking	Up to three months
Mysost	Scandinavian Countries	Light brown; sweetish taste. Imported is made from goat's milk; domestic from cow's milk	Eating	Six to eight months
Parmesan	Italy	Dark green or black surface; whitish inside. Hard, granular texture. Flavor gets stronger with age. Very old Parmesan is a delicacy	Eating when new Grating	Up to several years
Pineapple	United States	A Cheddar type, shaped like a pineapple	Eating Cooking	Six to eight months

A CHEESE CHART OF THE BEST-KNOWN VARIETIES (*Cont'd*)

Cheese	Origin	Characteristics	Use	How long it may be ripened
Oka Port du Salut	Canada France	Russet surface; creamy inside. Semihard. Mild flavor between Brick and Limburger. Made by Trappist monks	Eating	Five to six weeks
Sap Sapo	Switzerland	Green throughout. Hard and pungent-flavored with herbs. Small, conical shape	Eating Grating	Six months to two years
Sbrinz	Switzerland	Grayish-green surface; white inside. Hard texture and medium-sharp flavor	Grating	Six months to two years
Stilton	England	Wrinkled surface; creamy with green mold veins inside. Semihard texture; sharp flavor	Eating	Six months to two years

Swiss	Switzerland	Brownish-yellow surface with thick rind; light yellow interior with regular holes. Semihard; nutty flavor	Eating Cooking Grating	Three months to two years
Tilsit	East Prussia Germany	Yellowish outside; white to yellow inside.	Mostly eating Sometimes cooking	Four to six months
Primost	Norway	Soft, light brown, mild flavor. Unripened; made from whey	Eating	Not at all
Provolone Mozzarella (Sometimes called Scamorze)	Italy	Mozzarella is the fresh variety; it is white, rubbery, with a slightly acid taste. Provolone is hard with a yellow-brown surface and yellowish inside. Sharp, smoky flavor. The kind of cheese that is link-shaped or round, and hangs from strings	Eating Cooking Grating	Up to one year

A CHEESE CHART OF THE BEST-KNOWN VARIETIES (*Cont'd*)

Cheese	Origin	Characteristics	Use	How long it may be ripened
Romano	Italy	Greenish-black surface; whitish inside. Granular and hard texture; sharp flavor	Grating	Two years
Ricotta	Italy	White, soft, like cottage cheese	Eating Cooking	Not at all
Roquefort	France	Foil-wrapped; green mold veins inside. Semihard texture. On the crumbly side; sharp flavor. Made from ewe's milk. Only genuine Roquefort is allowed to have the name Roquefort. Imports are marked Roquefort—France	Eating Cookin	Three to nine months

Appetizers & Canapés

ARMENIAN CHEESE CRISPS Old Mrs. Seklemian makes these crisps in California, just as her mother and grandmother made them in the Old Country many years ago.

3 cups sifted flour	¾ lb. (3 cups) new, soft
¾ cup cold water, about	Cheddar, Mozzarella, or
2 tsp. oil	Monterey Jack cheese
1 tsp. salt	chopped parsley
cornstarch	melted butter

Mix flour, water, oil, and salt with fork into ball of dough. Cover with a damp cloth and leave at room temperature for about 1 hour. Lightly cover baking board with cornstarch. Roll out dough and divide into 4 parts. Roll each section as thin as paper. Place thin slices of cheese on each section and sprinkle with parsley. Fold over each section to make a package. Pinch edges together very firmly. Place in buttered baking dish. Cover with melted butter. Bake in moderate oven 25 to 30 minutes, or until crisp and well browned. Makes 16 crisps. They're excellent as a snack with beer.

PARMESAN SALAD CRISPS   One of the nicest cheese biscuits.

½ cup butter
½ cup grated Parmesan
   cheese

1 cup flour
½ tsp. baking powder
½ tsp. salt

Cream butter until soft. Add Parmesan cheese. Mix until well blended. Add flour which has been sifted with baking powder and salt. Roll out thin on lightly floured board. Cut into rounds about 1 inch in diameter. Place on baking sheet. Bake in hot oven for 8 to 10 minutes, or until slightly brown. Cool, and put crisps together with the following filling:

Filling:

2 tbs. butter
¼ cup grated Parmesan
   cheese

2 tbs. cream

Cream butter until soft. Beat in Parmesan cheese and cream. Mix until well blended. Makes 8 to 10 servings.

CHEESE FINGERS

1 cup sifted flour
½ tsp. salt
dash pepper

1½ cups (6 ozs.) grated
   sharp Cheddar cheese
4 tbs. softened butter
2 tbs. milk, about

Sift together flour and seasonings. Add cheese and butter. Mix with fork until crumbly and well blended. Gradually stir in milk until moist enough to roll. Roll on slightly floured board about ⅛ inch thick. Cut into finger lengths. Place on greased baking sheet. Bake in hot oven about 10 minutes, or until slightly brown. Makes about 3½ dozen fingers, depending on size.

CAMEMBERT SHORTBREAD Strange to the uniniti-
ated; but the initiated come back for more, with their beer.

¼ cup butter	*¼ cup grated Swiss cheese*
3 portions (3-oz.) Camem-	*3 eggs*
bert cheese, which must	*1 tsp. salt*
be ripe	*2 cups sifted flour*

Cream butter until soft. Blend in Camembert, rind included, and Swiss cheese. Add eggs, one at a time, beating
well after each addition. Stir in salt and flour. Mix until
soft dough is formed. Pat out on lightly floured board into
circle 10 inches in diameter. Place on greased baking sheet.
Cut into 16 pie-shaped wedges. Bake in hot oven 25 to 30
minutes, or until brown on top.

Variation: For a more pungent flavor, 3 ounces Lieder-
kranz or 3 ounces Limburger may be substituted for the
Camembert.

MISS THELMA'S CHEESE SHORTCAKES Thelma
Walker has red hair and the distinction of being one of the
few advertising copywriters who can cook as well as they
can write about food. She serves these shortcakes with
potent cocktails, and everybody eats them up as fast as they
come.

1 package Borden's Pippin Roll or ½ cup grated very sharp
   Cheddar
½ cup butter   *1 cup flour, about*
¼ tsp. Worcestershire Sauce

Cream cheese and butter until soft. Whip in Worcestershire Sauce. Gradually add flour, mixing until a smooth,
soft dough is formed. Chill for about half an hour. Roll
into small balls. Place on lightly greased baking sheet. Bake
in hot oven for 10 minutes. Serves 4.

DUTCH CHEESE NIPS

1 3-oz. package cream cheese	1 cup sifted flour
½ cup butter	½ tsp. salt

Have cheese and butter at room temperature. Mix until creamy, gradually adding flour and salt. Mix until well blended. Remove from bowl, wrap in wax paper, and chill overnight. Roll on lightly floured board into rectangle. Cut into any desired shapes. Place teaspoon of filling on pastry. Cover with another piece of pastry. Pinch edges together with fork. Brush top with cream. Place on baking sheet and bake in hot oven 15 to 18 minutes, or until done. Makes 8 or more.

Fillings   1. Mix ½ pound liverwurst with 1 tablespoon finely chopped onion.

2. Mix 1 cup grated Cheddar cheese with 1 tablespoon softened butter, 1 tablespoon finely chopped parsley, and 1 teaspoon prepared mustard.

3. Mix 1 cup cottage cheese with 1 tablespoon caraway seeds, 1 tablespoon finely chopped onion, and ½ teaspoon salt.

TOASTED CHEESE ROLLS

1 (3-oz.) package cream cheese	½ tsp. salt
2 tbs. butter	dash white pepper
1 tbs. chopped parsley	8 thin slices fresh bread

Soften cheese and blend with butter, parsley, and seasonings until creamy. Spread on bread. Remove crusts from bread and carefully roll the slices. Secure with toothpicks. Cover with damp napkin or towel and let stand in cool place until ready to bake. Place on greased cookie sheet and bake in moderate oven until brown, about 10 to 13 minutes. Makes 8 rolls.

QUICK CHEESE BREAD   Good with all casseroles and salads.

Remove all crust but the bottom one from a loaf of unsliced white or rye bread. Cut lengthwise through center to ½ inch of the bottom. Cut crosswise into 1½- to 2-inch slices. Brush all surfaces with melted butter. Sprinkle generously with grated sharp Cheddar or Parmesan cheese. Bake on greased cookie sheet in moderate oven until slightly brown. Serve hot. Serves 8 or more.

TEA PARTY TREATS

bread
1 (3-oz.) package cream
* cheese*
2 tbs. butter

2 tbs. powdered sugar
½ tsp. cinnamon
¼ tsp. vanilla

Cut bread into desired shapes. Cream together cheese, butter, sugar, cinnamon, and vanilla. Spread on bread. Place on greased cookie sheet and bake in moderate oven until slightly brown, or about 10 to 12 minutes. Serves 4.

CHEESE MELTAWAYS   Fluffy as a cloud in June.

2 egg whites
½ tsp. salt
⅛ tsp. white pepper
dash Worcestershire Sauce

1 cup (¼ lb.) grated sharp
* Cheddar cheese*
fine white cracker crumbs
fat for deep frying

Beat egg whites until stiff. Fold in salt, pepper, Worcestershire Sauce, and cheese. Form into small balls and roll in cracker crumbs until well coated. Fry in deep fat (365° F.) 2 or 3 minutes, or until golden brown. Makes about 15 balls, depending on size. Serve on toothpick.

This mixture is quite soft, so be sure that each ball is well covered with crumbs and that the fat is deep enough to cover balls completely.

CHEESE BALLS

1 3-oz. package cream
   cheese
¼ cup crumbled Blue
   cheese

½ tsp. Worcestershire Sauce
½ cup chopped walnuts
2 tbs. finely chopped parsley
   or walnuts

Blend cream and Blue cheese. Add Worcestershire Sauce and walnuts. Form into balls and roll in finely chopped parsley or walnuts. Makes 6 or more small balls.

BLUE CHEESE BALLS

½ cup Blue cheese
4 tbs. butter
1 tsp. Worcestershire Sauce
1 tsp. chopped chives or
   grated onion

dash of cayenne
pumpernickel crumbs or
   chopped nuts

Cream together Blue cheese and butter until well blended and smooth. Add seasonings. Mix well. Shape mixture into balls and roll in pumpernickel crumbs or finely chopped nuts. Serves 4.

KAAS BLOKJES (LITTLE CHEESE BLOCKS)   A Dutch appetizer. Cut Dutch cheese (or any other sharp cheese) into cubes. Sprinkle generously with celery salt. Serve on toothpicks.

RAW MUSHROOM CANAPÉ   As nice to eat as they are careful of a lady's figure.

Wash mushrooms. They should be on the small side. Remove stems, and save for soup or sauce. Make holes in caps slightly larger. Fill with ½ teaspoon any cheese spread or cottage cheese mixed with chives and well seasoned.

CHEESE BONBONS Any of the cheese spreads may be slightly chilled, rolled into balls, and put between halves of pecans or walnuts. Chill before serving.

STUFFED CELERY Wash and scrub celery. Separate into pieces. Use any of the fillings below—they are but a few examples of the many varieties of celery fillings.

Stuffed Celery I

1 package process American   *2 tbs. catsup or chili sauce*
    cheese   *½ tsp. celery seeds*

Soften cheese at room temperature. Blend in sauce. Add celery seeds. Mix well.

Stuffed Celery II

¼ lb. (1 cup) Blue cheese   *4 tbs. finely chopped salted*
1 tbs. butter   *peanuts or almonds*

Soften cheese at room temperature. Blend in butter. Mix until creamy. Add nuts. Mix well.

Stuffed Celery III

1 3-oz. package cream   *1 tbs. finely chopped parsley*
    cheese   *1 tbs. minced onion or*
2 tbs. cream   *chives*

Soften cheese at room temperature. Blend in cream until fluffy. Add parsley and onion. Mix well.

These mixtures may also be used as toppings for crisp crackers, melba toast, or potato chips. Garnish with sliced stuffed olives, sprigs of parsley, or paprika.

Soups

CHEESE IN SOUPS Practically all soups are very much improved if they are served with plenty of grated cheese. It adds enormously to the flavor of vegetable soups, such as celery, potato, spinach, tomato, etc. Grated cheese is essential with the mixed vegetable soup the Italians call Minestrone.

The best grating cheese for the purpose is Parmesan, next, Romano. If you don't have any on hand, the little cartons of grated cheese put out by Borden, Kraft, and other cheese companies will do.

Here are a few famous French soups where Parmesan is used:

Consommé Florentine This is a clear chicken broth with a small amount of rice boiled in it, served with plenty of grated Parmesan cheese on the side.

Consommé Parmesan A clear consommé with Parmesan Salad Crisps served on the side.

Consommé Viennoise This is a clear consommé with cheese pancakes cut into thin strips (julienne-wise) in it.

CHEESE ASPARAGUS SOUP

1 tbs. butter
1 tbs. flour
2 cups milk
1 cup cooked asparagus,
   chopped or mashed

1 tsp. salt
dash white pepper
¾ cup grated Cheddar
   cheese

Melt butter. Remove from heat. Blend in flour and gradually add milk, stirring until well blended. Cook over low heat, stirring constantly, until thick and smooth. Add asparagus and seasonings. Mix well. Just before serving, add cheese. Stir until cheese is melted and well blended. Makes 4 small servings.

Variation   Instead of asparagus, you can use 1 cup mashed potatoes.

SIMPLE CHEESE SOUP   The kind of soup one turns to when life is too much—it's the equivalent of a bowl of bread and milk, and quite as good to cry into.

½ cup butter
½ cup flour
2½ cups boiling water
1 tsp. salt
dash pepper

dash of nutmeg
1 cup (¼ lb.) grated cheese
   (any kind will do, but
   Swiss is best)

Cook butter and flour until golden and bubbly. Take care not to brown. Add boiling water, salt, pepper, and nutmeg. Stir until smooth. Simmer for half an hour. Before serving, add cheese. Stir well. Serve very hot. Serves 4.

Variation   This soup can be enriched by using consommé or bouillon cube stock instead of water. It is even richer if, before serving, and *after* it has been taken off the stove, the beaten yolk of 1 egg is stirred into it.

CREAM OF CHEESE SOUP A nice soup for a cold winter's night.

1 large onion	*1 tsp. salt*
2 cups water	*2 cups milk*
2 tbs. butter	*at least ½ cup grated*
2 tbs. flour	*Parmesan cheese*

Slice onion into water. Cook in water 10 to 15 minutes until tender. Drain, saving onion liquid. Melt butter. Remove from heat. Blend in flour and salt. Gradually add milk and onion liquid. Cook over low heat, stirring constantly, until thickened and smooth. Add cheese and stir until melted. Serve hot with crisp crackers. Makes 4 servings.

FRENCH ONION SOUP Perhaps *the* classic French soup—wonderfully comforting to mind and innards. And it's so easy to make with the simplest ingredients you are bound to have in the house.

½ to ¾ cup butter	*1 quart hot consommé or*
1 to 2 lbs. sliced onions, de-	*stock made from 4 bouil-*
pending on whether you	*lon cubes*
like a thinner or thicker	*salt and pepper*
soup	*Croutons or toast slices*
1 to 2 tbs. flour	*at least 1 cup grated Parme-*
	san cheese

Melt butter in saucepan, taking care not to brown. Add onions, and cover. Cook over low heat until onions are soft and golden, stirring occasionally. The onions must not brown. Sprinkle flour on onions. Add hot consommé. Stir well. Season. Simmer gently for 1 hour. Serve with fried croutons and grated Parmesan cheese. Or else place triangles of toast or slices of French bread on soup and sprinkle with grated Parmesan cheese. Place in hot oven until cheese is melted. Serve with additional Parmesan cheese. This soup is better when it's reheated. Serves 4.

CHEESE, TOMATO, AND ONION SOUP

2 cups sliced onions
3 tbs. butter
6 fresh tomatoes cut into quarters or 1 cup canned tomatoes
salt and pepper

a sprinkling of orégano or your favorite herb
1½ pints (3 cups) consommé, or stock made from 3 bouillon cubes
1 cup (¼ lb.) grated Parmesan cheese

Cook onions in butter until tender and golden. Add tomatoes and cook 5 minutes longer. Add seasoning, herb, and consommé or stock. Simmer for 10 minutes, or until tomatoes are cooked. Strain. Before serving, add grated cheese. Serves 3 to 4.

CHEESE AND CABBAGE SOUP

1 small cabbage, shredded
1 large potato, peeled and sliced
1 qt. milk

3 tbs. butter
salt and pepper to taste
1 cup (¼ lb.) grated Swiss or Parmesan cheese

Cook cabbage and potato until soft in as small an amount of salted water as possible. Drain, and mash coarsely with a fork. Add milk and butter. Season. Cook carefully over low heat for 10 minutes, taking care that the vegetables don't burn. Before serving, add grated cheese. Serves 4.

AUSTRIAN CHEESE SOUP   A nice, simple dish from the Austrian Tyrol.

½ cup butter
½ cup flour
1 tsp. salt
dash pepper
4 cups hot water

1 cup (¼ lb.) grated Cheddar, Swiss, or Parmesan cheese
4 tbs. chopped chives or parsley, if desired

Melt butter. Remove from heat. Blend in flour, salt, and pepper. Gradually stir in hot water, mixing until smooth. Cook over low heat, stirring constantly, until thick and smooth. Cover. Simmer over low heat for 20 minutes, stirring occasionally. Add cheese. Blend well. Serve in warm soup plates or petites marmites. Garnish each serving with 1 tablespoon chopped chives or parsley. Serves 4.

CHEESE CRUMB DUMPLINGS

1 egg, slightly beaten   *½ cup grated cheese*
⅛ tsp. salt   *¾ to 1 cup fine soda-*
dash pepper   *cracker crumbs*
1 tsp. finely chopped parsley *1 or 2 qts. hot soup*

To egg and remaining ingredients add enough crumbs to make a·mixture that will hold its shape. Drop by half teaspoonfuls into rapidly boiling consommé or any other soup. Cover, and simmer 10 minutes. Makes about 24 dumplings.

PANATA   Panata means made with bread. It's a very old dish—it goes way back to the fourteenth century.

¼ lb. stale bread, or 1 cup   *½ cup grated Parmesan*
*   dry bread crumbs*   *   cheese*
4 eggs, well beaten   *4 cups hot stock or*
½ tsp. salt   *   consommé*
dash of nutmeg

Grate bread coarsely and mix with eggs, salt, nutmeg, and cheese. Place in saucepan. Stir in 1 cup of the hot stock or consommé. Stir mixture constantly, keeping it in a ball in center of saucepan. Fill tureen with remaining consommé. Add mixture, which, if it has been made correctly, should separate into small bunches when added to the hot soup. Makes 4 servings.

SUPA SHETGIA   This is hardly a liquid soup, though, whatever it is, the taste is really good. The inhabitants of the Engadine eat it in that part of Switzerland in which St. Moritz is located.

2 slices stale rye bread,	*salt*
toasted **or** *2 slices stale*	*dash pepper*
French bread, toasted	*dash nutmeg*
4 tbs. grated Swiss cheese	*1 tbs. butter*
⅓ cup boiling milk	

Place 1 slice bread in soup plate or deep serving plate. Cover with cheese. Top with another slice of bread. Pour milk over bread. Cover dish and let stand 5 minutes. Remove cover. Season with salt, pepper, and nutmeg. Lightly brown butter. Pour over bread. Makes 1 serving.

HENRIETTE   SEKLEMIAN'S   EXCELLENT   LEEK SOUP

5 leeks, sliced	*salt and pepper*
4 tbs. washed, uncooked	*1 cup (¼ lb.) grated Swiss*
rice	*cheese*
3 cups chicken broth or	*1 cup white wine*
stock made from bouillon	
cubes	

Put leeks and rice into saucepan. Add water just to cover. Simmer 20 minutes, or until rice is tender. Add chicken broth or stock. Let come to a boil. Season to taste. Melt cheese with wine in top of double boiler. Mix well. Put a good spoonful of the cheese sauce in each serving of soup. Makes 4 or 5 servings. Crisp French bread is good with this soup.

ITALIAN   PARMESAN   SOUP   (STRACCIATELLA)
A soup from Italy that's beloved by old and young. Strac-

ciatella means "ragged"—you'll see why when you make the soup.

2 to 4 tbs. grated Parmesan cheese

1 cup fresh bread crumbs

2 eggs, slightly beaten

1 qt. (4 cups) hot consommé, or stock made from 4 bouillon cubes

salt and pepper to taste

Mix cheese, bread crumbs, and eggs. Gradually stir into consommé, which must be boiling. Season. Simmer for 8 to 10 minutes, stirring constantly. The cheese-bread-crumbs-eggs mixture will become like so many tiny rags. Serve with more grated Parmesan cheese. Serves 4.

Hot Breads, Biscuits, & Muffins

CHEESE MUFFINS

2 cups sifted flour	1 egg
3 tsp. baking powder	3 tbs. melted shortening,
1 tsp. salt	cooled
1 cup (¼ lb.) grated Ameri- can cheese	1 cup milk

Sift flour. Measure, and sift again with baking powder and salt. Add ¾ cup cheese. Mix well. Combine egg, shortening, and milk. Stir into dry ingredients, mixing with a fork until just blended. Mixture will be moist and lumpy. Do *not* mix until smooth. Fill greased muffin pans ⅔ full, sprinkle with remaining cheese, and bake in hot oven 20 to 25 minutes until done and brown. Makes 12 to 16 muffins, depending on size.

Variation: This mixture may also be poured into a greased 8-inch ring pan. Bake in hot oven 20 to 25 minutes, or until done and browned. The ring may be served with creamed deviled eggs, creamed chicken or beef, or creamed vegetables.

CHEESE HIDEAWAYS   Prepare mixture as for Cheese Muffins, omitting grated cheese. After filling muffin tins, press 1 inch cubes of Cheddar or Swiss cheese in center of each muffin. Cover with batter. Bake as directed.

BLUE CHEESE FANTANS

2 cups sifted flour
3 tsp. baking powder
1 tsp. salt
4 tbs. shortening

¾ cup milk
1 cup (¼ lb.) Blue cheese,
    room temperature
2 tbs. butter, softened

Sift flour. Measure and sift again with baking powder and salt. Cut in shortening with 2 knives or pastry blender until mixture seems coarse and crumbly. Stir in milk, mixing gently with a fork until soft dough is formed. Toss on lightly floured board. Knead gently 10 times. Roll into rectangle 8 by 12 inches. Cut lengthwise into strips. Mix together butter and cheese until soft and creamy. Spread 3 strips with cheese. Put all strips together sandwich fashion. Cut into 12 pieces. Place in greased muffin pans. Brush tops with cream. Bake in hot oven 15 to 18 minutes, or until done. Makes 12 fantans.

CHEESE POPOVERS

1 cup flour
½ tsp. salt
1 cup milk

2 eggs, slightly beaten
1 cup (¼ lb.) finely grated
    Cheddar cheese

Sift dry ingredients together. Add milk, eggs, and cheese. Beat with rotary egg beater until well blended and bubbly. Butter cold custard cups or muffin pans. Fill half full of batter. Place in cold oven. Start heat at 425° F. for 20 minutes, then reduce heat to moderate 350° F. and bake 20 to 25 minutes longer. Makes 12 to 16 popovers, depending on size.

SAGE CHEESE BISCUITS

2 cups sifted flour
3 tsp. baking powder
1 tsp. salt

1 cup (¼ lb.) sage or other
cheese, finely diced
2 tbs. shortening
¾ cup milk, about

Sift flour. Measure and sift again with baking powder and salt. Add sage cheese. Mix well. Cut in shortening with 2 knives or pastry blender. While doing this, cheese is also cut a little finer. Stir in milk with a fork until soft dough is formed. Toss on lightly floured board and knead gently 10 times. Roll ½ inch thick. Cut with biscuit cutter. Place on ungreased baking sheet, about ¼ inch apart for crisp sides. Brush lightly with cream, if desired. Bake in hot oven 12 to 15 minutes, or until done. Makes 12 to 16 biscuits, depending on size.

CHEESE SPOON BREAD A great improvement over a wholesome but not very interesting dish.

1 cup corn meal
1½ tsp. salt
½ tsp. dry mustard
dash of cayenne

3 cups milk, scalded
1 cup (¼ lb.) grated sharp
Cheddar cheese
3 eggs, well beaten

Mix corn meal, salt, mustard, and cayenne. Gradually stir into scalded milk, stirring constantly to avoid lumps. Cook until mixture thickens. Remove from heat, add cheese, and stir until melted. Add eggs. Pour into buttered 2-quart baking dish. Bake in moderate oven about 35 to 40 minutes. Makes 4 to 6 servings.

Variation: Follow above recipe, but separate eggs. Blend well-beaten egg yolks into corn-meal mixture. Fold in egg whites which have been beaten until stiff but not dry. Proceed as above.

CHEESE WAFFLES

2 cups sifted flour
2 tbs. sugar
3 tsp. baking powder
1 tsp. salt
1 cup (¼ lb.) grated cheese

2 eggs, separated
1½ cups milk
¼ cup melted butter,
    cooled

Sift flour. Measure and sift with dry ingredients. Add cheese and mix well. Combine well-beaten egg yolks with milk and butter. Pour into dry ingredients. Mix until just blended. Fold in stiffly beaten egg whites. Bake on hot waffle iron. Serve hot with scrambled or creamed eggs, creamed vegetables, chicken, et cetera. Makes 6 to 8 waffles.

GALETTES   A French way of doing waffles. Galettes are good with wine or drinks, or with fresh fruit.

1 cup sifted flour
1 tsp. salt
1 cup (¼ lb.) grated sharp
    cheese

2 eggs, well beaten
1 cup milk
fat for deep frying

Mix flour, salt, and cheese. Beat eggs and add milk. Pour on the dry ingredients and mix until smooth. Drop by teaspoonfuls into deep, hot fat (365° F). As soon as the galettes are in the fat, separate the batter with 2 forks. This gives them a lacy, uneven appearance, and makes them crisp. Makes 4 or more servings.

CHEESE LUNCH TOAST

2 eggs beaten
1 cup milk
1 cup grated Cheddar or
    Parmesan cheese

1 tsp. salt
dash pepper
8 slices stale bread

Mix eggs, milk, cheese, and seasonings. Dip bread in egg and cheese mixture and fry in butter until browned on one side. Turn to finish browning. Serve with a salad or with butter and apricot jam. Makes 4 servings.

Fondues, Soufflés, Puddings, & Rabbits

BRILLAT-SAVARIN'S CLASSIC FONDUE

Brillat-Savarin, French gastronome and the greatest writer about food, said that "a meal without cheese is like a pretty woman with only one eye." This is the master's version of one of the world's great dishes.

1 egg per person. Weigh the eggs

⅓ of the egg's weight in Swiss cheese

⅙ of the egg's weight in butter

salt and pepper

Grate cheese. Break eggs into a saucepan, beat, and mix as for a French omelet. Add butter in small pieces, stirring. Add cheese, and stir until everything is well mixed. Now place saucepan on a brisk—I do mean brisk—fire and stir constantly until mixture begins to thicken. It should be the consistency of a thick cream that can just be eaten with a fork. Serve at once on a warm, not hot, plate, else the mixture overcooks.

Fondue, however creamy, must always be eaten with a fork. At least that's what people say who care for tradition. Personally, I think it also tastes good eaten with a spoon—but then I like the easy way.

THE TRUE SWISS FONDUE This is the classic Swiss recipe, as good here as in Switzerland. I give you the version of the Switzerland Cheese Association, because I couldn't possibly improve on it. Try it, and you'll understand why poets have sung of this fondue.

For this dish you will need:

1 earthenware casserole holding about 4 cups, or a chafing dish, or a similarly shaped cooking utensil with a handle.

1 alcohol stove the flame of which is easily adjustable; or any electric plate, with an asbestos pad, that will hold the cooking utensils securely.

These are the ingredients for 2:

½ lb. (2 cups) Switzerland Swiss cheese, shredded
1½ tbs. flour
1 clove garlic
1 cup Neuchatel wine (or any light dry wine of the Rhine, Riesling or Chablis types)
salt, pepper, and nutmeg
1 loaf French or other crusty bread, or at least 4 hard rolls cut into bite-size pieces each of which must have at least one side of crust
3 tablespoons Kirschwasser or 2 tablespoons brandy, applejack, light rum, or other non-sweet brandy. (Optional, but very desirable)

Dredge cheese with flour. Rub the cooking utensil with the garlic. Pour in the wine and set over very slow fire. When the wine is heated to the point that air bubbles rise to the surface (it must not boil), stir with a fork and add the cheese by handfuls, each handful to be completely absorbed and dissolved before another one is added.

Keep stirring until the mixture starts bubbling lightly. At this point add a little salt and pepper and a dash of nutmeg (optional). Finally add and thoroughly stir in the Kirschwasser or other brandy. Remove the bubbling fondue from the fire and set immediately on your preheated table-heating equipment.

Spear a piece of bread with a fork, going through the soft part first and securing the points in the crust. The idea is not to lose your bread when you dip it into the fondue (first loser pays for the works is often the rule). Dunk the bread in a stirring motion until your neighbor takes over to give you a chance to enjoy your morsel. While each one takes his leisurely turn, his stirring will help maintain the proper consistency of the fondue and will assure that each piece is thoroughly coated with melted cheese.

Care should be taken that the fondue keeps bubbling lightly. This is done by regulating the heat or by turning it off or on. If the fondue becomes a little too thick at any time, this can be rectified by stirring in a little preheated— never, never cold—wine. Toward the end, some of the melted cheese will form a brown crust at the bottom of the utensil. When that happens, keep the heat low in order to prevent the utensil from cracking. The crust can easily be lifted out with a fork and is considered to be a special delicacy.

NOTE: Omit cold or iced drinks during the meal. To those who like it, a pony of Kirschwasser or brandy may be served. But all should finish with a cup of hot coffee or hot tea.

AMERICAN FONDUE

2 cups milk
2 cups dry bread cubes
1 tsp. salt
½ tsp. dry mustard

⅛ tsp. pepper
2 cups (½ lb.) grated Ched-
dar or Swiss cheese
4 eggs, separated

Scald milk. Add bread cubes, seasonings, and cheese. Cook over low heat, stirring constantly, until cheese is melted. Slowly pour the cheese mixture over well-beaten egg yolks. Stir until well blended. Cool. Beat egg whites until stiff but not dry. Fold into cheese mixture. Pour into buttered 1½-quart baking dish. Bake in moderate oven 50 minutes, or until set. Makes 4 to 6 servings.

FONDUE FROM FRIBOURG   A Swiss fondue that's easy and quick. The cheese must be soft yet tasty—like the "vacherin" cheese of the original.

2 tbs. butter	*2 tbs. hot water*
1 clove garlic, crushed	
1 lb. (about 4 cups) Gold-	
N-Rich cheese, cut into	
cubes	

Melt butter. Add garlic, and cook 2 minutes. Remove from heat. Remove garlic from butter. Add cheese and cook over low heat. Stir with fork until smooth and creamy. Gradually add water. Mix well. This fondue needs very low heat and constant careful stirring. Makes 4 servings.

POTATO SOUFFLÉ

2 cups hot mashed potatoes	*2 tbs. butter*
½ cup hot milk	*1 tbs. finely chopped parsley*
½ cup grated Cheddar	*(optional)*
cheese	*4 eggs, separated*

Prepare mashed potatoes as usual. Beat in hot milk, cheese, butter, and parsley. Beat egg yolks until thick and lemon-colored, about 5 minutes. Beat egg whites until stiff but not dry. Fold egg yolks into potato mixture, then fold in egg whites. Pile lightly in buttered baking dish. Bake in hot oven 20 to 25 minutes, or until puffed and lightly browned on top. Makes 4 servings.

CHEESE SOUFFLÉ This excellent soufflé was developed by the Kraft Foods Company—another example of the fine recipes produced by American food companies. It is a little drier than a French soufflé, but it does not collapse too quickly, and stands up well for an elegant effect.

4 tbs. butter	*1½ cup milk*
4 tbs. flour	*½ lb. "Old English" Pasteur-*
1 tsp. salt	*ized Process cheese, sliced*
dash cayenne	*6 eggs, separated*

Melt butter in top of double boiler placed over boiling water. Remove from boiling water and blend in the flour, salt, and cayenne. Gradually add the milk, blending well. Return to boiling water and cook, stirring constantly, until the sauce is thick and smooth. Add sliced cheese and continue cooking, stirring frequently, until cheese has melted. Remove from heat and slowly add the beaten egg yolks, blending them in well. Slightly cool mixture, then pour it slowly onto the stiffly beaten whites of eggs, cutting and folding thoroughly together. Pour into ungreased 2-quart casserole.

Run the tip of a teaspoon around in the mixture one inch from the edge of the casserole, making a slight "track" or depression. This forms the "top hat" on the soufflé as it bakes and puffs up.

Bake 1¼ hours in a slow oven. Serve immediately. Serves 4.

SOUFFLÉ FLORENTINE

3 tbs. butter	*1 cup (¼ lb.) grated Ched-*
4 tbs. flour	*dar cheese*
½ tsp. salt	*1 cup finely chopped cooked*
dash pepper	*spinach, well drained*
dash nutmeg	*3 eggs, separated*
1 cup milk	

Melt butter. Remove from heat. Blend in flour and seasonings. Gradually add milk, stirring until well blended. Cook over low heat, stirring all the time until thick and smooth. Add cheese and spinach. Blend well. Cook until cheese is melted. Cool. Beat egg yolks until thick. Add to spinach mixture. Beat egg whites until stiff but not dry. Fold into spinach mixture. Pour into buttered 1½-quart baking dish. Bake in slow oven about 50 to 60 minutes. Serves 4.

FRENCH CHEESE SOUFFLÉ

2 tbs. butter	dash pepper
2 tbs. flour	4 eggs, separated
1½ cups milk	1 cup (¼ lb.) grated Swiss
salt	or Gruyère cheese

Melt butter. Add flour and blend. Add milk, stirring all the time until mixture is smooth. Season. Cook for 5 minutes, or until mixture bubbles. Remove from heat. Add slightly beaten egg yolks and cheese. Beat egg whites until stiff but not dry. Fold into mixture. Pour mixture into individual buttered baking dishes. Bake in moderate oven 10 to 15 minutes. Makes 4 to 6 servings, depending on the size of individual baking dish.

This dish can also be made in a 1½-quart buttered baking dish. For the diamond-top effect you see in fancy restaurants, cut thin diamonds of Swiss or Gruyère cheese. Place them on soufflé *before* baking.

CRÈME LORRAINE A lovely dish from France—lighter and more delicate than a soufflé.

6 slices bacon	2 cups heavy cream
1½ cups (6 ozs.) grated	2 eggs, well beaten
Swiss or Gruyère cheese	1 tsp. salt
1½ cups (6 ozs.) grated	¼ tsp. white pepper
Parmesan cheese	

Fry bacon until crisp. Break into small pieces. Mix with cheese, cream, eggs, and seasonings. Pour into 1½-quart baking dish. Bake in moderate oven 35 to 40 minutes, or until set. Makes 4 servings.

PARMESAN PUDDING A flavorsome, nutritious main dish.

6 eggs, separated　　　　*dash pepper*
¼ cup flour　　　　*1 cup (¼ lb.) grated Par-*
1 cup milk　　　　　*mesan cheese*
salt

Beat egg yolks and stir in flour. Add milk and seasonings. Cook until mixture is thick, stirring all the time. Add cheese and cook until cheese is melted, stirring constantly. Grease a mold. Pour mixture into mold. Cover tightly and steam for ¾ hour in pan of hot water on top of stove. Take care that the water in the pan is not boiling, but keep it just at the simmering point, or your pudding will be watery and full of holes. Unmold. Serve with additional grated Parmesan cheese. This pudding tastes good with a tomato or mushroom sauce. Serves 4.

STEAMED CHEESE PUDDING One of the nicest dishes made with cheese. Serve it with creamed vegetables, chicken, or mushrooms, or just by itself with a crisp salad.

¼ cup butter　　　　　*1 cup flour*
4 eggs, separated　　　*1 tsp. salt*
2 cups (½ lb.) grated　　*dash pepper*
　cheese (half Swiss, half
　Parmesan)

Cream butter until soft. Add egg yolks and beat until creamy; this will take about 5 minutes. Stir in cheese, flour, and seasonings. Mix well. Add stiffly beaten egg whites. Pour into buttered 8-inch mold. Cover. Place in pan half full of simmering water on top of stove. Steam for about 35 to 40 minutes, or until done. Take care that the water is kept at the simmering point. If it boils, the pudding will be watery and have holes. Carefully loosen sides of pudding and unmold on hot platter. Serve with additional grated cheese. Serves 4.

FROMAGE

2 egg yolks   salt
½ cup milk   pepper
2 cups (½ lb.) grated Ched-
    dar or Swiss cheese

Beat egg yolks until light and lemon-colored, about 5 minutes. Blend in milk, cheese, and seasonings. Pour into 4 greased custard cups. Bake in slow oven 15 to 20 minutes, or until set and browned on top. Makes 4 servings.

This is a rich dish which has a nutlike flavor if made with Swiss cheese and a sharper, tangier flavor, if made with Cheddar cheese.

CHEESE CUSTARD

¼ lb. Cheddar or cheese   ¼ tsp. Worcestershire
    food   Sauce
1½ cups scalded milk   2 eggs, slightly beaten
dash pepper   hot buttered spinach
¾ tsp. salt

Cut cheese into small pieces. Add to scalded milk with seasonings and stir until blended. Pour over eggs, mixing well. Pour into 4 buttered custard cups set in pan of hot water. Bake in slow oven for 40 minutes, or until a knife inserted in center comes out clean. Unmold on a bed of hot, buttered, chopped spinach. Serves 4.

WELSH RABBIT I

2 tbs. butter
¾ tsp. salt
½ tsp. dry mustard
⅛ tsp. pepper
¾ lb. (3 cups) sharp Cheddar cheese, grated or slivered fine

¾ cup beer or ale
1 egg, well beaten

Melt butter. Add seasonings and cheese. Cook over low heat, stirring all the time until cheese is melted. Stir in beer or ale. Mix well. Just before serving, quickly stir in egg. Makes 4 servings.

WELSH RABBIT II

4 tbs. butter
4 tbs. flour
1 bouillon cube, broken into pieces
1 tsp. salt
½ tsp. prepared mustard

2 cups milk
½ lb. (2 cups) sharp Cheddar cheese, grated or slivered fine
2 tbs. sherry wine, if desired

Melt butter. Remove from heat and blend in flour, bouillon cube, and seasonings. Add milk slowly, blending well. Cook over low heat, stirring constantly, until thick and smooth. Add cheese and cook until melted and well blended. Just before serving, stir in sherry wine. Serve hot on toast, toasted soft rolls, or toasted English muffins. Makes 4 to 6 servings.

CHEESE AND LEEK PIE Henriette Seklemian loves leeks and knows many ways of fixing them. Here's my favorite—a main dish men are partial to.

Boil some leeks. When done, cut into 1-inch lengths—there should be enough to cover an 8-inch pie shell.

Pour about 2 cups Cheese or Mornay Sauce into pie shell. Arrange leeks on top of sauce. Cover leeks with about 1 to 1½ cups sliced Swiss or grated Parmesan cheese. Bake in slow oven for 15 to 20 minutes, or until set.

If you want to omit the pie shell, bake leeks and sauce in buttered shallow baking dish. Serves 4.

ORIGINAL SWISS CHEESE PIE

piecrust for 9-inch pie
½ lb. (2 cups) Swizerland
  Swiss cheese, grated
1 tbs. flour

3 eggs, well beaten
1 cup milk or light cream
salt
pepper

Line pie plate (it must be a deep one) with pastry. Chill. Dredge cheese with flour. Place cheese evenly on pastry. Mix eggs with milk and seasonings. Pour mixture over cheese. Bake 15 minutes in hot oven, then reduce heat to slow oven, and bake an additional 30 minutes, or until knife inserted in center of pie comes out clean. Serve hot or warmed over, never cold. Serves·4.

Variation   Instead of making a large cheese pie, you may use the above ingredients for small, individual tartlets. Proceed as above, but bake in hot oven for 20 to 25 minutes only. Serve hot or warmed over, never cold.

Fish

CHEESE AND FISH OR SEA FOOD **1.** Arrange fillets of white fish in a buttered shallow baking dish. Cover with a custard (2 eggs to 1 pint of milk and ½ cup grated Swiss cheese). Sprinkle with more grated Swiss cheese. Bake until custard is set.

2. Cover a buttered shallow baking dish with a purée of mushrooms or thin slices of mushrooms. Place layer of fillets of white fish or leftovers of cooked and flaked white fish over mushrooms. Cover with Cheese Sauce and bake until golden crisp.

3. Cook and flake smoked finnan haddie. Place on toast and cover with Cheese Sauce. Broil until Cheese Sauce is brown. Or else bake finnan haddie (which must be cooked) with cheese sauce in a moderate oven until brown.

4. Salt cod, cooked and flaked, is much more interesting if baked in oven with a cheese sauce.

5. Cooked and flaked lobster is excellent served with Mornay Sauce. So are steamed clams or mussels. Or try baking them with a simple Cheese Sauce.

6. Mix sliced hard-cooked eggs and cooked flaked fish. Spread on toast. Place on greased baking sheet. Cover with cheese sauce. Top with sliced Swiss cheese. Broil until cheese is melted.

SCALLOPED FISH AU GRATIN Haddock, flounder, or any leftover flaked fish may be used.

1 lb. cooked fish	*½ tsp. salt*
¼ cup butter	*3 tbs. flour*
¼ cup diced green pepper	*1½ cups milk*
2 tbs. diced onion	*½ cup grated cheese*
½ tsp. Worcestershire Sauce	*½ cup soda cracker crumbs*

Cut fish into cubes or flakes. Melt butter. Add green pepper, onion, Worcestershire Sauce, salt, and fish. Sauté over low heat about 10 minutes, stirring frequently. Remove from heat. Blend in flour. Gradually add milk. Cook over low heat, stirring constantly, until slightly thickened. Pour into buttered 1½-quart casserole. Mix grated cheese and cracker crumbs and spread over the top. Bake in moderate oven until brown and bubbly, or about 15 to 20 minutes. Makes 4 to 6 servings.

SUPERIOR CODFISH CAKES

1 recipe codfish cakes to serve 6	*½ to ¾ cup grated Cheddar cheese*

Blend cheese into codfish mixture. Cook as usual.
Variation: Fish loaves and timbales may be served with Cheese Sauce or Mornay Sauce.

CRAB MEAT À LA DEWEY

1 lb. cooked crab meat   1 recipe Mornay Sauce
1 tbs. lemon juice

Flake crab meat. Remove membranes and discard them. Sprinkle with lemon juice. Place in shallow individual baking dishes or crab shells. Cover with sauce. Place on middle shelf of broiler and broil until top is brown and bubbly. Serves 6.

CRAB MEAT SUPRÊME

1 lb. cooked crab meat   1 cup light cream
¼ cup butter   1 egg yolk
3 tbs. flour   ½ cup dry white wine
½ tsp. salt   ⅓ to ½ cup mild grated
dash of pepper   Cheddar or Swiss cheese

Break crab meat into flakes. Remove hard membranes and discard them. Melt butter. Remove from heat. Blend in flour and seasonings. Gradually add cream, mixing until smooth and well blended. Cook over low heat, stirring constantly, until thick and smooth. Add 2 tablespoons of the hot liquid to the egg yolk. Mix well. Add to remaining hot liquid. Cook over low heat 3 minutes longer. Add wine and cheese, stirring until cheese is melted. Add crab meat. Mix well. Pour into buttered individual baking dishes or 1½-quart buttered baking dish. Sprinkle with additional cheese. Bake in hot oven 5 to 8 minutes, or until cheese is browned. Make 6 servings.

Cooked cleaned shrimps, lobster, or scallops may be used in place of crab meat.

FLORENCE'S FISH GRILL This dish can be made with any kind of fish: split whole cleaned fish, or fish steaks or fillets of any fish. It may be necessary to increase other ingredients according to the type of fish.

1 lb. fillet of flounder   *2 tomatoes, peeled and*
salt and pepper to taste   *diced*
1 tbs. grated onion   *butter*
                                          ½ cup grated Swiss cheese

Wash fish. Drain and place in buttered shallow baking dish. Sprinkle with salt, pepper, and grated onion. Place diced tomatoes on top of fish. Dot with butter. Place under medium broiler heat. Cook until fish will flake slightly—20 minutes. Sprinkle with cheese. Return to broiler and cook until cheese is melted. Makes 4 servings.

BAKED FILLETS OF FISH MORNAY

1 lb. fillets of flounder or   *butter*
   other fish   *1 cup Mornay Sauce*
salt and pepper to taste

Wash fish. Drain and place in buttered shallow baking dish. Sprinkle with salt and pepper. Dot with butter. Bake in moderate oven until fish flakes or is done—about 20 minutes. Pour *hot* Mornay Sauce over fish. Place under broiler. Cook until golden brown and bubbly. Makes 4 servings.

For a simpler dish, substitute a cheese sauce for the Mornay Sauce.

ENGLISH FISH AND CHEESE PIE   Good for people who don't like to eat fish.

1 lb. boiled flaked haddock   *salt and pepper*
   or other white fish   *½ cup grated Parmesan or*
3 cups sliced parboiled   *Swiss cheese*
   potatoes   *butter (⅛ lb.)*
2 cups Cheese Sauce

Arrange alternate layers of fish, potatoes, and Cheese Sauce in a buttered deep baking dish. Season. The last 2 layers should be potatoes and Cheese Sauce. Dot with butter; sprinkle with grated cheese. Bake in moderate 'oven until top is crisp and golden brown. Serves 4.

BAKED HALIBUT WITH SUPRÊME SAUCE

2 lbs. halibut	*1 tsp. salt*
1 tbs. lemon juice	*¼ tsp. pepper*
1 tsp. onion juice	*¼ cup melted butter*
(optional)	*flour*

Clean, bone, and cut halibut in fillets. Combine lemon juice, onion juice, salt, and pepper. Dip fillets in butter and roll up. Fasten with toothpicks. Put in shallow baking pan, and sprinkle with mixed juices then with flour. Bake in hot oven 20 to 30 minutes. Serve with Suprême Sauce. Makes 4 to 6 servings.

Suprême Sauce

3 tbs. butter	*¼ lb. (1 cup) Cheddar*
3 tbs. flour	*cheese, grated*
1½ cups light **cream**	*2 tbs. sherry wine*
½ tsp. salt	*2 hard-cooked eggs, sliced*

Melt butter. Remove from heat. Add flour, blending well. Add cream gradually. Add salt. Cook over low heat until thick, stirring constantly. Add cheese and mix well. Stir in sherry. Arrange halibut on platter and cover with sauce. Garnish with slices of hard-cooked eggs.

COQUILLES ST. JACQUES The most elegant of fish and cheese combinations, and surprisingly easy to make.

1 lb. fresh scallops	1 tsp. salt
juice of 1 lemon	¼ tsp. pepper
2 cups water	1 cup rich milk or cream
1 tbs. butter	2 egg yolks
1 bay leaf	½ cup grated Swiss cheese
2 tbs. butter	2 tbs. sherry wine
2 tbs. flour	paprika

Wash scallops. If large, cut into pieces. Sprinkle with lemon juice. Simmer in water with 1 tablespoon butter and bay leaf for 5 minutes. Drain. Melt the 2 tablespoons butter. Remove from heat. Blend in flour, salt, and pepper. Gradually add milk or cream, mixing until smooth and well blended. Cook over low heat, stirring constantly, until thick and smooth. Beat in eggs and cheese. Cook 3 minutes longer. Add sherry and scallops. Pour into buttered ramekins or scallop-shaped baking dishes. Sprinkle with paprika. Bake in moderate oven 15 to 20 minutes, or until top is slightly brown. Makes 4 to 6 servings.

TUNA FISH WITH NOODLES AND CHEESE

1 (13-ounce) can tuna fish	1 recipe Cheese Sauce
2 cups cooked medium noodles	½ cup buttered bread crumbs
2 tbs. finely chopped olives (optional)	

Flake tuna and drain it. Arrange alternate layers of tuna and noodles in greased baking dish. Sprinkle each layer with olives. Add cheese sauce. Sprinkle top with buttered bread crumbs. Bake in moderate oven about 25 minutes, or until brown on top. Makes 6 servings.

Meat & Poultry

CHEESE IN MEAT DISHES **1.** Meat loaf, hamburger, or hash (homemade or canned) take on a delightful flavor if ½ cup grated cheese is added to each pound of meat before cooking. The cheese can be Parmesan, Swiss, Cheddar, or any cheese that will grate.

2. Leftover meat is good if it is cut into dice and baked in a moderate oven with a Cheese Sauce. Count about 1 cup sauce for 2 cups of meat.

3. Another way of using leftover meat is to cut it into dice. Add diced cheese—the proportion is 1 part of cheese to 2 parts of meat. Bind with tomatoes, canned, fresh, or juice. Bake in moderate oven until cheese is melted.

STEAK SMOTHERED WITH CHEESE

A rich and handsome combination, well liked by any gentleman I have tried it on.

Broil steak as usual. When almost done, cover with slices of sharp Cheddar cheese. Return to broiler and cook until cheese is melted.

FILLET OF PORTERHOUSE À LA ROQUEFORT

New, and very delicious if you're tired of steak the old way.

Take an individual fillet of porterhouse or any other steak. Broil 2 minutes on both sides. Cut 1-inch squares halfway through steak on top sides—about 3 or 4 for each steak, depending on size. Press 1 heaping teaspoon grated or crumbled Roquefort cheese into slits. Return to broiler and broil to taste. Serve very hot. Makes 1 serving.

Variation Treat lamb chops in the same way—the number of slits depending on the size of the chops. Blue cheese can also be used for both these dishes.

STUFFED HAMBURGERS

1 lb. ground beef	4 to 5 slices of Cheddar
¼ tsp. pepper	cheese or cheese food
1 tsp. salt	

Lightly mix meat and seasonings. Form into 8 or 10 thin patties. Put the patties together sandwich fashion with the cheese in between. Make sure that cheese is securely sealed between meat, to avoid seeping out. Broil on one side, turn, and finish broiling on other. Makes 4 or 5 hamburgers.

CHEESEBURGERS Broil hamburgers on one side. Turn. Spread undone side with mustard and top with thick slices of cheese. Broil until cheese is melted and brown.

Variation: Thick slices of tomato may be placed on the cheese and broiled.

Or mushroom caps may be placed on the cheese and broiled.

FANCY BEEF OR VEAL BIRDS

*1½ lbs. top-round beef or
  veal steak
salt
pepper
poultry seasoning
8 ½-in. sticks Cheddar or
  Gold-N-Rich cheese*

*flour
4 tbs. fat
1 onion, diced
1 cup canned tomatoes,
  tomato sauce or con-
  sommé*

Pound meat until thin. Cut into 8 slices. Sprinkle with salt, pepper, and poultry seasoning. Place cheese on each piece of meat. Roll and tie with string, making sure that the cheese is well covered. Roll in flour. Melt fat. Cook onion until tender in fat. Remove onion. Brown meat rolls in fat on all sides. Drain off excess fat. Add tomatoes, sauce or consommé. Cover. Simmer 20 to 25 minutes, or until done. Makes 4 servings.

STUFFED FRANKFURTERS

*2 ¼-in.-thick slices of
  Cheddar or cheese food
4 frankfurters*

*prepared mustard
4 slices bacon*

Cut each slice of cheese into 4 pieces. Split frankfurters lengthwise, but not quite through. Spread cut sides with mustard. Place 2 pieces of cheese into each frankfurter. Wrap with bacon. Hold together with toothpicks. Place on lowest shelf of broiler and broil under low heat for 8 to 10 minutes, or until bacon is crisp and cheese melted. These frankfurters may also be cooked over an open picnic fire. Serves 4.

CHEESE BEEF CUTLETS WITH WINE A dish for meat-and-gravy lovers, so be sure to serve it with dry rice or with noodles and plenty of crisp bread.

1½ lbs. top-round beef-
steak cut into ¼-in.-thick
slices
½-in. slices of Swiss or
Cheddar cheese, as many
as there are slices of meat
salt
pepper

2 tbs. butter
1 medium-sized onion,
diced
1 cup consommé or stock
made with 1 cup water
and 2 bouillon cubes
½ cup dry white wine

Cut slices into serving-size pieces, and cut cheese into same size pieces. Sprinkle meat with salt and pepper. Sauté in butter with onion. Brown both sides. Add consommé. Cover. Simmer until tender. Top each piece of meat with cheese. Cover. Cook 3 minutes. Add wine and simmer 5 minutes longer. Thicken gravy if desired. Makes 4 to 6 servings.

SWISS MEAT SANDWICHES

1¼ lbs. top-round steak
salt
pepper
4 ⅛-in. slices Swiss cheese

milk
bread crumbs
suet or shortening

Cut meat into 8 thin slices. Sprinkle with salt and pepper. Cut cheese just a little smaller than size of meat. Put cheese between 2 slices of meat, sandwich fashion. Tie securely so that cheese is completely covered. Dip in milk. Roll in bread crumbs. Sauté in hot fat until brown on one side. Turn, and continue cooking until done. Be sure that the cheese is well covered, otherwise it will seep out. Makes 4 servings.

AUSTRIAN CHEESE AND HAM CAKE   A dish from Innsbruck, where I had it on a hot summer's day with a crisp green salad.

3 tbs. butter
2 eggs, separated
¾ cup grated Parmesan
  cheese

1 cup finely diced, cooked
  ham
1 tsp. mustard

Cream butter until soft. Beat in egg yolks until mixture is fluffy and well blended. Stir in Parmesan, ham, and mustard. Fold in egg whites beaten until stiff but not dry. Pour into buttered 8-inch piepan. Bake in moderate oven until puffy and slightly brown on top. Cut into 4 or 6 wedges.

SWISS HAM TARTS

1 recipe rich, flaky pie pastry
¾ cup milk, scalded
1 tbs. chopped chives
  (optional)
¼ tsp. salt
dash pepper

dash nutmeg
2 eggs, slightly beaten
½ cup grated Swiss cheese
1½ cups ground cooked
  ham

Line 6 tart shells with pastry. Chill. Add milk and seasonings to beaten eggs. Add cheese and ham. Fill tart shells to the top. Bake in hot oven 15 minutes, then lower heat to moderate and bake 15 to 20 minutes longer, or until a knife inserted in center comes out clean. Makes 6 tarts.

GRILLED HAM AND SWISS CHEESE

prepared mustard
8 thin slices boiled ham

8 ½-in. sticks Swiss or
  Cheddar cheese

Spread mustard on ham. Place cheese on ham. Roll and secure with string or toothpicks. Place on boiler rack, place on lower shelf of broiler, and broil under medium heat. Turn until browned on all sides. Makes 4 servings.

Variation Bologna slices may be used in place of ham.

HAM HÔTELIÈRE   A wonderful party dish—easy and very impressive.

4 slices cold boiled ham,   ½ cup Mornay Sauce
   about ⅛ inch thick   ½ cup grated cheese
½ cup thick Mornay Sauce   2 tbs. butter
1 cup thick tomato sauce,
   well seasoned

Spread slices of ham with thick Mornay Sauce. Roll and secure with toothpicks. Pour tomato sauce into bottom of shallow 8-inch baking dish. Place ham rolls on sauce. Cover with ordinary Mornay Sauce. Sprinkle with cheese. Dot with butter. Bake in a moderate oven about 15 minutes, or until golden brown. Serves 4.

CHEESE AND HAM TARTS

1 recipe pie pastry   1½ cup milk
2 tbs. butter   1 cup (¼ lb.) grated Ched-
2 tbs. flour   dar or Swiss cheese
½ tsp. salt   1 cup finely diced boiled
dash pepper   ham

Line 6 individual tart shells with pastry. Chill. Melt butter and remove from heat. Blend in flour and seasonings. Gradually stir in milk until mixture is smooth. Cook until thick. Add ¾ cup of the cheese. Stir until cheese is melted. Add ham and mix well. Fill chilled tart shells. Sprinkle with remaining cheese. Bake in hot oven 20 to 25 minutes, or until pastry is golden and top is brown and bubbly. Makes 6 tarts.

HAM À LA BELGIQUE

4 stalks Belgium endive   1 recipe Easy Cheese Sauce,
butter   warm
4 slices boiled ham

Wash endive and remove wilted leaves. Drain. Sauté in butter on all sides until lightly browned. Roll each stalk in slice of boiled ham. Pour some of the sauce in greased baking dish. Place endive and ham bundles on sauce. Cover with remaining sauce. Bake in moderate oven 30 to 35 minutes, or until bubbly and brown. The endive will be pleasantly crisp, not soft. Makes 4 servings.

HAM AND CHEESE CUSTARDS A delicate dish that's good for invalids.

*1½ cups ground cooked
  ham
½ cup grated Cheddar
  cheese*

*¾ cup scalded milk
2 eggs, slightly beaten*

Mix ham and cheese. Stir milk gradually into eggs. Pour over ham-and-cheese mixture. Mix well. Pour into 4 buttered custard cups or timbale molds. Place in pan of hot water and bake in moderate oven 30 to 35 minutes, or until a knife inserted in center comes out clean.

These custards may also be gently steamed on top of the stove by placing them in a pan of hot water and covering well. Cook about 35 minutes. The top will not be brown. Serves 4.

VEAL CHOPS LUCULLUS

*4 veal chops cut 1 inch
  thick
salt
pepper
4 thin slices ham*

*4 thin slices Swiss, Gold-N-
  Rich, or Gruyère cheese
butter or shortening
hot water*

Make pocket in each veal chop. Sprinkle with seasonings. Insert ham and cheese in pocket. Secure with toothpicks. Brown on both sides in hot fat. Remove excess fat. Add hot water. Cover. Simmer until chops are tender. If desired, thicken gravy. Makes 4 servings.

VEAL CUTLETS PARMESAN   An Italian dish beloved by Americans, to judge from the many times it's ordered in Italian restaurants.

½ tsp. salt
dash pepper
2 eggs, well beaten
3 tbs. grated Parmesan
  cheese
bread crumbs
4 veal cutlets

butter
½ lb. semisoft cheese, such
  as Mozzarella (prefer-
  ably), Munster, Gold-N-
  Rich, or other of the kind,
  sliced

Add salt and pepper to the eggs. Mix grated cheese with bread crumbs. Dip cutlets in eggs and then in bread crumbs. Fry in butter on both sides for about 5 minutes, or until almost done. Cover cutlets with slices of cheese. Place under broiler until cheese is melted. Serve very hot. Tomato sauce is good with this dish. Makes 4 servings.

Variation   A simpler dish is prepared by leaving out the slices of cheese and broiling.

On the other hand, a richer dish is obtained by placing a slice of cooked ham under the slices of cheese before broiling.

VEAL OR LAMB STEW AND CHEESE DUMPLINGS

favorite veal or lamb stew,
  hot
2 cups sifted flour
4 tsp. baking powder
1 tsp. salt

4 tbs. grated Cheddar
  cheese
1 tbs. butter
1 cup milk

Sift flour. Measure and sift again with baking powder and salt. Stir in cheese. Cut in butter with knife. Add milk, stirring quickly with a fork to form a soft dough. Drop by teaspoonfuls on top of hot stew on the range, being sure that dough rests on vegetables and meat and that it does not sink into the liquid. Cover tightly. Simmer 20 minutes. Serve at once. Serves 4 to 6.

VEAL À LA VALDOSTANA   Veal itself is a bland meat, that's why it needs dressing up, as in this fine company dish.

4 tbs. butter	*slices of boiled ham*
1 tbs. anchovy paste, or	*slices of Swiss cheese*
pounded anchovy fillets	*1 egg, slightly beaten*
1½ lbs. veal cut thin as for	*1 tbs. water*
scaloppine	*flour*

Mix butter with anchovy paste. Spread on half the thin veal slices. Cover each piece of meat with a slice of boiled ham and cheese. Cover with another slice of veal, sandwich fashion. Secure with toothpicks or strings, taking care that all of the cheese is well covered, to avoid it seeping out. Dip meat sandwiches in egg mixed with water and then in flour. Sauté in hot fat until browned on all sides. Serve very hot. Serves 4.

VEAL À LA MORNAY   Another rich, festive dish.
Sauté very thin slices of veal cut as for scaloppine. Take care that the slices are of about the same size and that you have an even number of them. Spread half the meat with thick Mornay Sauce. Top with remaining slices sandwich fashion. Secure with toothpicks. Place in shallow buttered baking dish. Cover with melted butter. Sprinkle generously with grated cheese. Place under broiler to heat through and brown.

Variation Leftover roast beef, veal, or lamb may be used in place of veal. Proceed as above.

Leftover meat loaf may be sliced thin and treated in the same manner.

A DIFFERENT LEFTOVER MEAT CASSEROLE

2 cups diced or sliced left-
over cooked meat
salt
pepper
1 cup (½ pint) sour cream

1 cup (¼ lb.) grated Ched-
dar or Swiss cheese
2 medium-sized onions
cut into thin rings

Arrange alternate layers of meat sprinkled with salt and pepper, sour cream, cheese, and onions in buttered 1½-quart baking dish. Bake in moderate oven 25 to 30 minutes, or until bubbly and heated through. Makes 4 servings.

CHICKEN HASH MORNAY Good for late, lazy Sunday breakfasts.

2½ cups chopped cooked
chicken
1 cup chopped cooked
mushrooms

1 recipe Mornay Sauce
½ cup grated Cheddar
cheese or cheese food

Mix chicken, mushrooms, and Mornay Sauce. Place in 6 buttered individual baking dishes. Sprinkle with the cheese. Broil under medium heat until slightly brown. Makes 6 servings.

CHICKEN AND BROCCOLI SUPRÊME For each serving, place sliced cooked chicken on toast. Place one stalk of cooked broccoli on top. Cover with Mornay Sauce.

Sprinkle with paprika. Place under medium heat of broiler and broil until slightly brown. This is the sort of dish you find in fashionable restaurants.

TURKEY CASSEROLE

2 cups (2 8-oz. cans) tomato
*   sauce*
½ cup water
3 cups cooked spaghetti
1½ cups diced leftover
*   turkey or other cooked*
*   meat*

½ lb. (2 cups) Cheddar or
*   cheese food, diced*
salt and pepper

Mix tomato sauce and water. Arrange alternate layers of spaghetti, turkey, sauce mixture, and cheese in buttered 1½-quart baking dish, making top layer cheese. Sprinkle each layer lightly with salt and pepper. Bake in moderate oven 25 minutes, or until heated through and top is slightly brown. Makes 4 to 6 servings.

Eggs

CHEESE WITH EGGS Any egg dish is called Florentine if it contains spinach and Mornay Sauce or Cheese Sauce. The eggs may be cooked any way for a Florentine dish.

CHEESE WITH OMELETS

Basic Cheese Omelet Make your favorite omelet, allowing 2 tablespoons grated cheese for each egg. You can use any kind of grateable cheese, but remember that each cheese has a different flavor. Salt lightly, as the cheese is salty. Pour egg mixture into pan. Sprinkle the cheese over it evenly. Cook as usual. Be sure heat is low.

Cheese Omelet with Roe Before folding cheese omelet, add sautéed fish roe.

Cheese Omelet with Finnan Haddie Mix together 1 cup Thin Cream Sauce and 1 cup cooked, flaked finnan haddie. Make 6-egg cheese omelet. Before folding, add fish mixture.

Creole Cheese Omelet   To a 6-egg cheese omelet add 1 cup Thick Creole Sauce before folding.

Mushroom Cheese Omelet   Proceed as for Basic Cheese Omelet. After sprinkling cheese over egg mixture in pan, sprinkle over cheese 1 cup sliced, sautéed mushrooms. This quantity is sufficient for 6 eggs.

NOTE   Cheese omelets are more successful if they are made as described, rather than adding the cheese to the uncooked egg mixture, that is to the eggs that you have beaten in a bowl.

PUFFY COTTAGE CHEESE OMELET

4 eggs, separated
½ cup top milk or light
  cream
¾ cup cottage cheese

2 tbs. finely chopped parsley
  or chives (optional)
1 tsp. salt
¼ tsp. pepper
1 tbs. butter

Beat egg yolks with milk or cream, cheese, parsley or chives, and seasonings. When well blended, fold in egg whites beaten until stiff but not dry. Melt butter in frying pan. Pour omelet in pan. Cook over low heat until bottom is browned. Finish cooking in moderate oven 15 to 20 minutes, or until brown on top. Makes 4 servings.

HEARTY CHEESE OMELET

4 eggs
1 tsp. salt
1 cup of your favorite
  cheese, diced (the cheese
  should be soft, not dry)

1 tbs. butter
2 tbs. grated cheese

Beat eggs slightly with salt. Add cheese to eggs. Heat butter in skillet. Pour in egg-and-cheese mixture. Lift edges and let unset egg run into bottom of pan. When mixture has set, sprinkle with grated cheese. Serves 4.

CREAM CHEESE OMELET

*1 3-oz. package cream
  cheese
3 tbs. heavy cream
2 tbs. chopped parsley or
  chives*

*¼ tsp. Worcestershire Sauce
1 tsp. salt
dash pepper
4 eggs, separated
butter*

Mix cream cheese with cream until smooth and free of lumps. Add parsley or chives, Worcestershire Sauce, and seasonings. Slightly beat egg yolks. Mix egg yolks with cheese mixture, blending well. Whip whites stiff but not dry. Heat butter in skillet, taking care that the sides are well buttered. Pour omelet into skillet which must be hot. Lower heat, and cook omelet until bottom is cooked. Place skillet under medium broiler and cook until top is browned. Serve hot and immediately. Tomato sauce goes well with this omelet. Serves 2 to 4.

CHEESE SAUSAGE OMELET

*½ lb. sausage meat
4 eggs
4 tbs. milk
½ tsp. salt*

*dash pepper
½ cup Gold-N-Rich, Mel-
  O-Pure, Elmo, or similar
  semihard cheese, diced*

Cook sausage meat, breaking with fork, until well cooked. Drain off excess fat. Mix eggs, milk, salt, and pepper until well blended. Pour over sausage meat. Sprinkle cheese over mixture. Cook over low heat, loosening eggs from sides and letting unset mixture run to bottom of pan. Cook until set. Makes 4 servings.

SWISS SCRAMBLED EGGS

4 eggs   *1 tbs. butter*
½ tsp. salt   *4 to 6 slices Swiss cheese*
dash of pepper   *bread crumbs*
6 tbs. milk or light cream

Beat eggs well. Add salt, pepper, and milk or cream. Melt butter in saucepan, add egg mixture, stirring constantly until just thick *but not firm.* Pour into buttered shallow baking dish. Place cheese on top. Sprinkle with bread crumbs. Place in moderate oven or under broiler until cheese is melted and just slightly brown. Makes 4 servings.

SCRAMBLED EGGS DE LUXE

4 eggs   *½ cup grated Parmesan*
4 tbs. top milk or light   *cheese*
*   cream*   *4 slices buttered toast*
1 tsp. salt   *4 strips half-cooked lean*
1 tsp. Worcestershire Sauce   *bacon or Canadian bacon*
2 tbs. butter

Mix eggs, milk or cream, salt, and Worcestershire Sauce until eggs are well broken up. Melt butter in top of double boiler over hot water. Add eggs and cheese. Cook, stirring constantly, until of custardlike consistency. Spread on toast. Top with bacon and broil under medium heat until bacon is crisp. Makes 4 servings.

BAKED EGGS WITH CHEESE

Baked Eggs Country Style Place 2 tablespoons minced sauteed onion in individual baking dishes. Sprinkle lightly with grated Parmesan or Swiss cheese. Break eggs over onions. Season. Dot with butter. Sprinkle with additional cheese. Bake in moderate oven until eggs are set.

Eggs Florentine Place cooked, strained, buttered, and seasoned spinach on bottom of buttered baking dish or individual baking dishes. Break eggs on spinach. Cover with Mornay Sauce. Sprinkle with grated Swiss or Parmesan cheese. Broil under low flame until eggs are set. This dish can also be made with poached or hard-cooked eggs.

BAKED EGGS MORNAY

2 cups Mornay Sauce	*4 tbs. fine dry bread crumbs*
4 eggs	*4 tbs. grated Swiss cheese*
salt	*1 tbs. butter*
pepper	

Place ½ cup Mornay Sauce in 4 individual buttered baking dishes. Break egg carefully into sauce. Season. Sprinkle each serving with 1 tablespoon each bread crumbs and cheese. Dot with butter. Bake in moderate oven 15 minutes, or until whites are set. Makes 4 servings.

EGGS LUCERNE

½ lb. Swiss cheese, sliced	*about ⅓ cup top milk or*
4 eggs	*cream*
salt and pepper	*4 tbs. grated Swiss cheese*

Cover bottom of buttered shallow baking dish with sliced cheese. Break eggs over cheese. Season. Pour top milk or cream over eggs. Sprinkle with grated cheese. Bake in moderate oven for about 15 minutes, or until set. Serves 4.

SIMPLE BAKED EGGS

4 slices toast	*dash pepper*
butter	*grated Parmesan, Swiss, or*
4 eggs	*Cheddar cheese*
salt	

Butter toast and place in buttered shallow baking dish. Carefully break eggs on toast, taking care to keep the yolk whole. Season with salt and pepper. Sprinkle cheese generously over eggs and bake in moderate oven until eggs are set. Makes 4 servings.

POACHED EGGS WITH CHEESE

Creamy Poached Eggs   Poach 6 eggs in 1 cup of light cream. Place on hot platter. To the cream remaining in the pan add 2 tablespoons grated Swiss cheese, ½ teaspoon salt, dash of pepper, and, if desired, a dash of paprika. Stir until cheese is melted. Pour over eggs and serve hot with strips of toast. Makes 3 to 6 servings.

Poached Eggs Mornay   Arrange poached eggs in shallow baking dish. Cover with Mornay Sauce. Sprinkle with grated Parmesan cheese. Dot with butter. Place under broiler until brown.

Savory Poached Eggs   Place poached eggs on buttered toast. Cover with a thick tomato sauce. Dot with butter. Sprinkle generously with grated Swiss or Parmesan cheese. Broil until cheese is melted.

GLORIFIED EGGS

1 8-oz. package cheese food   *4 slices broiled or fried ham*
½ cup milk   *4 poached eggs*
2 English muffins, split and
*   toasted*

Cut cheese food into small pieces. Melt in top of double boiler. Add milk. Stir until well blended. Place ham on muffin halves. Top each with poached egg. Cover with hot sauce. Makes 4 servings.

HARD-COOKED EGGS WITH CHEESE

Farmers' Eggs Place alternate layers of sliced hard-cooked eggs and cheese sauce in buttered baking dish. Top with buttered crumbs. Bake in moderate oven until top is golden and bubbly.

This is a flexible dish. If you want to make it party fare, add layers of sautéed mushrooms, cooked asparagus, or peas.

Tomato Eggs Mornay Combine 1 cup Mornay Sauce, ¾ cup tomatoes, peeled and chopped, and 4 hard-cooked quartered eggs. Heat through over low fire. Do not boil. Take care that mixture does not stick. Serve on toast or boiled rice.

DEVILED EGGS WITH CHEESE SPREADS

6 hard-cooked eggs
½ jar smoky, Blue, sharp, or
*   any favorite cheese spread*
1 tbs. butter

1 tbs. heavy cream or
*   mayonnaise*
1 tsp. salt
⅛ tsp. pepper
6 stuffed olives, sliced

Remove yolks from whites. Blend with cheese, butter, cream or mayonnaise, salt, and pepper. Beat until creamy. Fill whites. Garnish with sliced stuffed olives. Serves 6.

DEVILED EGGS AU GRATIN

6 hard-cooked eggs
1 tbs. butter
1 tsp. salt
¼ tsp. pepper
¼ tsp. dry mustard
¼ tsp. prepared horse-radish

2 tbs. mayonnaise
4 slices bread, about
butter
1 cup (¼ lb.) grated
*   Cheddar cheese*

Cut eggs lengthwise. Remove yolks and mix with butter, salt, pepper, mustard, horse-radish, and mayonnaise until creamy. Fill whites with yolk mixture. Toast bread on one side. Butter untoasted side and place 3 halves of egg on each slice of bread. Sprinkle with cheese. Put on greased baking sheet and place under medium broiler until cheese is melted and slightly brown. Makes 4 servings.

BAKED LUNCHEON EGGS

¼ lb. sharp Cheddar cheese   12 halves deviled eggs
2 cups Medium White Sauce   12 tomato slices

Cut cheese into small pieces. Add to White Sauce. Cook over low heat, stirring constantly, until well blended. Arrange eggs on tomato slices in buttered shallow baking dish. Pour sauce over eggs and tomatoes. Bake in moderate oven 15 minutes, or until top is brown. Serves 4 to 6.

PIQUANT EGGS

½ lb. Cheddar or your   3 hard-cooked eggs, sliced
*   favorite cheese, chopped   hot rice, noodles, or 4 slices*
*   or sliced   toast*
1 10- or 11-oz. can con-   8 slices cooked bacon
*   densed tomato soup   (optional)*

Melt cheese in top of double boiler. Add tomato soup. Blend well. Add eggs. Heat thoroughly. Serve on well-seasoned rice, noodles, or toast. Garnish with bacon. Makes 4 servings.

Noodles, Rice, & Dumplings

CHEESE WITH SPAGHETTI, MACARONI, RICE, AND IN ALL ITALIAN DISHES As you know, the Italians use plenty of grated Parmesan or Romano cheese with their spaghetti, macaroni, and rice dishes. Cheese is an essential ingredient, and without it more than half of the taste would be lost.

Cheese adds flavor to boiled rice, to corn meal mush that has been fried, to fried hominy, and to homemade noodles. Cheese also provides needed proteins in simple, inexpensive meals made with spaghetti or macaroni.

In this book, I cannot even attempt to give you the variety of Italian dishes in which cheese is used. But remember, any dish of spaghetti and meat balls requires plenty of grated Parmesan or Romano—the more freshly grated, the better.

CHEESE RAVIOLI In Italy, the ravioli is made with Ricotta, a soft cheese. I make it with cottage cheese with the same excellent results.

Your favorite noodle dough

Filling:

2 cups (*1 lb.*) cottage
   cheese
1 cup (*¼ lb.*) grated
   Parmesan or Swiss cheese,
   or both mixed

3 egg yolks
1 tbs. chopped parsley or
   chives or grated onion
½ tsp. salt
dash pepper

Make your favorite noodle dough. It must be rolled very thin and spread on a clean cloth to dry. Cut into strips the length of the dough and about 3 inches wide. Mix all ingredients for the filling until smooth. Place a good ½ teaspoon of filling in dabs along the length of the dough near one edge. Keep the dabs about 1 inch apart. Fold the other edge of the dough over the filling, envelope wise. Cut into squares, cutting between the dabs of filling. Press edges *well together* with a fork or pastry crimper. Dry for about ½ hour. Drop these into plenty of boiling salted water. Cook 10 or 20 minutes, or until the paste is tender. Take up with skimmer and drain well. Serve with gravy, tomato sauce, or plenty of brown butter, and with lots of grated Parmesan. You can also bake cooked ravioli with Cheese Sauce in the oven or under the broiler. Serves 6 or more.

GNOCCHI ALLA ROMANA   A standby of Italian cooking—delicate, nourishing, and good as a main dish for lunches and suppers.

3 cups liquid (*half milk,*
   half water)
1 cup farina *or* Cream of
   Wheat
1½ tsp. salt
3 tbs. butter

3 eggs
2 cups (*½ lb.*) grated
   Parmesan or Swiss cheese
   (*Parmesan preferred*)
4 tbs. butter

Bring liquid to a boil. Gradually stir in farina and salt, taking care to avoid lumps. Cook until thick. Remove from heat. Beat in the 3 tablespoons butter, ½ cup cheese, and the eggs. Mix well. Spread about ¼ inch thick on shallow platter or tray. Cool. Cut into circles or any desired shape. Arrange in greased baking dish in layers. Sprinkle each layer with the remaining 1½ cups cheese and 4 tablespoons butter. Bake in moderate oven about 30 minutes, until golden crisp. Makes 4 to 6 servings.

STUFFED NOODLES (LASAGNE IMBOTTITE) A dish beloved by the Neapolitans—as excellent as it is nourishing.

2 lbs. broad noodles
2 to 2½ cups thick tomato
  sauce, or tomato and
  meat sauce
2 cups (1 lb.) Ricotta or
  cottage cheese

1 lb. (4 cups) cubed
  Mozzarella or Monterey
  Jack or Munster cheese
2 cups (½ lb.) grated
  Parmesan cheese
salt and pepper

This dish ought to be made with the Italian ingredients. However, they might not always be available. It comes out all right with the substitutes. Cook noodles according to directions on the package, until tender but not too soft. Drain. Put ½ cup tomato sauce on bottom of baking dish. Arrange alternate layers of noodles, grated Parmesan, tomato sauce, Mozzarella, and Ricotta. Add salt and pepper to each layer. The last layer should be tomato sauce and grated Parmesan. Bake in moderate oven until firm, or about 15 minutes. Serve in wedge-shaped pieces with more grated Parmesan. Serves 6 or more.

SPAGHETTI ALLA ALFREDO Alfredo made his restaurant in Rome famous with this dish. He made it with homemade noodles but spaghetti may be used. For favorite guests he would shake it up himself, with a flourish worthy of grand opera.

2 lbs. spaghetti or noodles	about 1 lb. (4 cups) freshly
½ lb. sweet butter, cut in small pieces	grated Parmesan cheese
	pepper

Cook spaghetti according to directions on the package, and be sure to have plenty of boiling water so it won't stick. Drain. Place in heavy saucepan that has a close-fitting lid. Add butter, cheese, and a little pepper. Close lid and shake the pan as hard as you can for several minutes. Serve at once on heated plates. If shaken sufficiently, the cheese and butter will have melted into a delicious creamy sauce. Serves 4 to 6.

KREPLECH OR JEWISH CHEESE RAVIOLI

1 recipe noodle dough	½ tsp. salt
1 lb. (2 cups) cottage cheese	½ tsp. powdered cinnamon
2 tbs. melted butter	grated rind of 1 lemon
1 egg	boiling milk or water
1 tsp. sugar	butter

Roll out noodle dough and cut into squares as for ravioli. Mix remaining ingredients. Place teaspoonful on each square of dough. Fold over and wet edges. Press firmly together. Drop into boiling milk or water. When done, they will rise to the top. Remove from liquid with skimmer or slotted spoon. Serve with melted butter. Serves 4.

CHEESE AND HAM SOUFFLÉ

½ 6-ounce package elbow macaroni	1 tbs. chopped parsley
	salt
½ cup ground cooked ham	3 eggs, separated
1 cup (¼ lb.) grated Cheddar or Swiss cheese	

Cook macaroni according to directions on box until tender. Drain. Mix with ham, cheese, parsley, and salt. Add well-beaten egg yolks. Fold in well-beaten egg whites. Pour into 1½-quart greased baking dish. Bake in moderately slow oven for 35 to 40 minutes, or until puffed and slightly brown. Makes 4 servings.

HAM AND NOODLES For a change try different cheeses in this dish. Each one will give it its own distinctive flavor.

2 cups cooked medium
   noodles (about 1 cup
   dry)
2 tbs. butter
2 tbs. flour
½ tsp. salt

dash pepper
2 cups milk
1 cup diced cooked ham
1 cup (¼ lb.) diced Swiss,
   Cheddar, Parmesan, or
   cottage cheese

Cook noodles according to directions on box until just tender. Drain. Melt butter. Remove from heat. Blend in flour and seasonings. Gradually add milk, mixing until well blended. Cook over low heat, stirring constantly, until thick and smooth. Remove from heat. Add ham and cheese. Add noodles. Pour into greased 2-quart casserole and bake in moderate oven 20 to 25 minutes, or until top is bubbly and slightly brown. Makes 4 to 6 servings.

COTTAGE CHEESE NOODLES These noodles taste like egg noodles, though they look pale. It's the protein in the egg and cottage cheese that gives that nice flavor.

¼ cup butter
½ cup (¼ lb.) cottage
   cheese
1 egg

½ tsp. salt
1¼ cups sifted flour

Cream butter until soft and fluffy. Beat in cottage cheese and egg until well blended. Stir in salt and flour. Mix well.

Roll very thin on floured board. Cut into any desired width. Dry thoroughly for several hours. Cook in lots of boiling salted water for 10 minutes. Drain. Serve with butter and grated cheese. Makes 3 to 4 servings.

BAKED EGGS AND SPAGHETTI

1 tbs. butter
1 tbs. flour
1 cup (1 8-oz. can) pre-
  pared tomato sauce
¼ cup water
½ to ¾ cup grated Cheddar
  cheese

1 tsp. salt
¼ tsp. pepper
2 cups hot cooked spaghetti
4 eggs
salt and pepper

Melt butter. Blend in flour. Gradually stir in tomato sauce and water. Mix until well blended. Cook over low heat, stirring constantly, until thick and smooth. Add cheese, salt, and pepper. Stir until cheese is melted. Place spaghetti in buttered shallow baking dish. Cover with sauce. Make 4 depressions in sauce and drop an egg in each one. Sprinkle lightly with salt and pepper and additional cheese, if desired. Bake in moderate oven 15 minutes, or until eggs are set. Makes 4 servings.

CHEESE BLINTZES

1 egg, slightly beaten
1 tsp. salt
1 cup water
1 cup sifted flour
butter
1 lb. (2 cups) cottage cheese
1 egg
1 tbs. melted butter

1 tbs. sugar
1 tsp. salt
½ tsp. powdered cinnamon
  (optional)
¼ cup chopped raisins
  (optional)
grated rind 1 lemon
sour cream

Mix egg, salt, and water. Stir in flour and mix until batter is smooth. Melt 1 teaspoon butter in 6-inch frying pan. Add 2 tablespoons batter to the pan and tilt so that the batter spreads out. Cook over low heat until cake is set and not brown on the bottom. Remove from pan and place on clean cloth. Fry remaining batter in the same way.

Mix cottage cheese and remaining ingredients (except cream) until well blended. Place a teaspoon of filling on each blintze. Fold over and press sides together well. Melt 4 tablespoons butter in a pan. Cook the blintzes in the butter until slightly brown on all sides. Serve with sour cream. Makes 10 to 12 blintzes, according to size.

BAKED RICE AND CHEESE

1 cup rice	*butter*
1 cup milk	*1 cup (¼ lb.) grated*
salt	*Cheddar cheese*
pepper	*bread crumbs*

Cook rice according to directions on package in boiling salted water for 15 minutes. Drain. Return to saucepan. Cover. Add milk. Continue cooking until soft and milk is absorbed, about 8 to 10 minutes longer. Arrange alternate layers of rice sprinkled with salt and pepper and dotted with butter and cheese in greased baking dish. Sprinkle top with bread crumbs, dot with butter, and bake in moderate oven until golden brown on top. Makes 4 servings.

Cooked leftover rice may also be used for a plainer dish.

BAKED CHEESE AND RICE CUSTARD

2 cups cooked rice	*1 tsp. salt*
1½ cups (6 ozs.) grated	*⅛ tsp. pepper*
Cheddar cheese	*¼ tsp. Worcestershire Sauce*
2 eggs	*(optional)*
3 cups milk, scalded	

Mix rice and cheese. Beat eggs slightly, gradually add milk, stirring until well blended. Add seasonings. Pour over rice and cheese. Pour into 1½-quart buttered baking dish or in buttered custard cups. Place in pan of hot water and bake in moderate oven for 45 to 50 minutes if in large dish, or 30 to 35 minutes for individual dishes. Makes 4 to 6 servings.

CHEESE AND RICE BALLS In Italy, where lots of cheese and rice are eaten, these balls are called "suppli," and eaten as snacks, with wine. They're fine as a main dish, utilizing leftover rice.

2 cups cooked rice
½ cup grated cheese
1 egg, well beaten
1 tbs. melted butter
2 tsp. prepared mustard
(optional)

1 tsp. salt
dash pepper
½-inch cubes of your favorite cheese
bread crumbs
fat for deep frying

Mix rice and grated cheese. Add egg and seasonings. Blend well. Cover each cube of cheese with the rice mixture. Form into balls. Dip into bread crumbs. Fry in deep, hot fat (365° F.) for 5 to 8 minutes, or until slightly brown on all sides. Makes 12 to 16 balls, depending on size.

When covering the cubes, be sure that there are no open places in the balls, so that the cheese won't seep out and separate from the rice.

RISOTTO AMERICAN FASHION

1 cup rice
1 medium-sized onion
3 tbs. butter
2 cups hot chicken broth or consommé or stock made from bouillon cubes

½ cup white wine
1 tsp. salt
dash pepper
1 cup (¼ lb.) grated Parmesan cheese

Wash and boil rice until water is clear. Drain. Cook onion in butter until soft and lightly browned. Add rice, and cook over low heat, stirring constantly, until golden brown in color. Add chicken broth, wine, salt and pepper. Cover tightly, and simmer over low heat about 20 minutes, or until all liquid is absorbed and rice is dry and fluffy. Heap on warm platter and sprinkle with Parmesan cheese. Makes 4 servings.

CHICKEN LIVER RISOTTO Follow recipe for Risotto, but add 6 cut-up chicken livers to onions while they are cooking. Before heaping on platter, mix in the Parmesan cheese. Serve with additional cheese.

Vegetables

VEGETABLES WITH CHEESE A great many vegetables are excellent if parboiled and then baked with Cheese Sauce or Mornay Sauce. I especially recommend the following vegetables treated in this manner:

Cabbage   Endives
Cucumbers   Spinach
Artichoke bottoms   Squash
Brussels Sprouts

The proportion is, roughly speaking 1 cup of Cheese Sauce or Mornay Sauce to every 2 cups of vegetables.

SPRINGTIME VEGETABLE PIE In our family we call it vegetables-without-tears because everybody comes back for seconds.

½ recipe pie pastry   ¾ tsp. Worcestershire Sauce
1 cup (¼ lb.) grated Ched-   (optional)
   dar cheese   2½ cups diced cooked
¾ cup milk, scalded   mixed vegetables
2 eggs, slightly beaten   2 tomatoes, peeled and cut
1 tsp. salt   into eighths

Prepare pastry as usual but blend ½ cup cheese into dry ingredients. Line 8-inch piepan with pastry. Chill. Bake in hot oven 10 minutes. Gradually add milk to eggs. Stir in salt, Worcestershire Sauce, and cooked vegetables. Pour into baked pie shell. Arrange tomatoes on top. Sprinkle with remaining cheese. Bake in moderate oven 35 minutes, or until set. Makes 4 to 6 servings.

ASPARAGUS PARMESAN   A simple way of serving asparagus, and one of the best.

hot cooked asparagus, fresh,   melted butter
frozen, or canned   grated Parmesan cheese

For each 6 stalks of asparagus you will need 1 tablespoon of melted butter and 2 tablespoons grated Parmesan cheese.

Arrange asparagus on serving plate. Pour melted butter over it. Sprinkle with Parmesan cheese. Serves 4.

Variation   Arrange layers of asparagus in shallow oblong baking dish or pan, the kind that's pretty enough to put on the table. Sprinkle with butter and grated cheese. Cover with another layer of asparagus, butter, and cheese. Bake in hot oven 4 or 5 minutes, or until cheese is slightly melted. Serve immediately.

FESTIVE ASPARAGUS

24 stalks cooked asparagus   ½ cup grated Cheddar,
4 slices boiled ham   Swiss, or Parmesan
1 cup Cheese Sauce or   cheese
*   Mornay Sauce*

Roll 6 stalks of asparagus in each slice of ham. Secure with toothpicks. Place in buttered shallow baking dish. Pour sauce over asparagus. Sprinkle with cheese. Bake in moderate oven 15 to 20 minutes, or until bubbly and slightly brown. Makes 4 servings.

Variations For a more complete meal, place each ham-asparagus bundle on a slice of toast. Or else 2 cups of fluffy buttered cooked rice may be placed in baking dish. Proceed as above.

CAULIFLOWER OR BROCCOLI PARMESAN Boil cauliflower or broccoli as usual until just tender. Break cauliflower carefully into flowerettes or leave whole. Broccoli is the right size. Place in buttered shallow baking dish which has been sprinkled with grated Parmesan cheese. Sprinkle generously with melted butter and more grated Parmesan. Bake in hot oven until slightly brown.

CHEESE AND CORN CASSEROLE This is a recipe that won a prize in a June Dairy radio contest, fully deserving it. And it's originator is a man, T. E. Reynolds, who's a chief steward on a ship!

2 cups (1 No. 2 can) cream-
  style corn
½ cup bread or cracker
  crumbs
½ cup milk
2 eggs, well beaten
1 tsp. salt

dash pepper
⅜ lb. (1½ cups) Gold-N-
  Rich cheese, grated or
  sliced
extra bread or cracker
  crumbs
butter

Mix all ingredients except cheese. Place in buttered baking dish. Cover top with grated or sliced Gold-N-Rich cheese. Sprinkle with additional bread crumbs and dot with butter. Bake in moderate oven for 35 minutes, or until set. Serves 4 or 5.

CELERY NUT CASSEROLE

4 cups cooked, drained, and diced celery	3 tbs. flour
¼ lb. (1⅓ cups) salted almonds or peanuts, coarsely chopped	1 tsp. salt
	dash of pepper
	2 cups milk
3 tbs. butter	1 cup (¼ lb.) grated Cheddar or Swiss cheese

Place celery in buttered baking dish and cover with nuts. Melt butter. Remove from heat. Blend in flour and seasonings. Gradually add milk, mixing until well blended. Cook over low heat, stirring constantly, until thick and smooth. Add cheese. Mix until blended. Pour over celery. Bake in hot oven 25 minutes, or until top is browned and bubbly. Serves 4.

Variation   Cook 2-inch sticks of celery in boiling water for 3 minutes. Drain. Place in sauce pan and cover with consommé or stock made with bouillon cubes. Add a small chopped onion and a few slices of ham or bacon, diced. Season. Cover and simmer until tender. Serve with hot melted butter and *plenty* of grated Parmesan cheese.

BAKED EGGPLANT WITH CHEESE   This is a dish you can make with different kinds of cheese. Depending on the cheese you use the taste will be sharper or milder. Personally, I prefer it with Parmesan, as done in Italy.

1 medium-sized eggplant	1 cup (¼ lb.) grated Cheddar, Swiss, or Parmesan cheese
salt	
1 egg	
4 tbs. milk	
1 tsp. salt	4 tomatoes, peeled and diced, or 1 cup tomato sauce
bread crumbs or flour	
butter or oil	

Wash eggplant, peel, cut into slices, sprinkle with salt, and let stand 1 hour. Drain off liquid. Mix egg, milk, and salt. Dip slices into egg mixture, then into bread crumbs or flour. Sauté in butter, oil, or other fat, until brown on both sides. Arrange alternate layers of eggplant, cheese, and tomatoes in buttered baking dish. The last layer should be cheese. Cover top with bread crumbs and dot with butter. Bake in moderate oven until heated through and brown on top. Makes 4 servings.

STUFFED GREEN PEPPERS

3 medium-sized green
*   peppers*
boiling water
1 to 1½ cups whole-kernel
*   corn*
1 egg
1 tsp. salt

½ tsp. Worcestershire Sauce
dash pepper
1 cup (¼ lb.) grated Ched-
*   dar, Swiss, or Parmesan*
*   cheese*
hot water or consommé

Wash peppers; cut in half lengthwise. Remove seeds and fibers. Cook in boiling water for 3 minutes. Remove from water and drain. Mix remaining ingredients. Stuff into peppers. Place in pan filled with water or consommé to depth of ¼ inch. Bake in moderate oven 25 minutes, or until set. Serves 3 to 6.

GREEN PEPPERS FIESTA   A very good and different way from Mexico, of doing peppers. The recipe there is made with a fresh, soft, local cheese. Fresh Monterey Jack is a suitable cheese, or Italian Mozzarella. If you don't have either, try Munster or a fresh Cheddar or similar cheese.

8 green peppers
salt
dash pepper

8 tbs. cheese
3 eggs, separated
fat for deep frying

Remove skin from green peppers by scalding or by holding over low heat until skin pops. Remove seeds and fibers by making a slit down one side of the pepper. Sprinkle inside with salt and pepper. Place 1 tablespoon cheese in each pepper. Secure openings with toothpicks. Beat egg yolks until thick and egg whites until stiff. Fold whites into yolks. Dip peppers into eggs. Fry in deep fat (375° F.) until brown on all sides. Serve hot with tomato sauce, chili sauce, or any other tart sauce. Serves 4 to 8.

LIMAS WITH A DIFFERENCE

1 package frozen lima beans
  or 1½ cup cooked limas
  (fresh or canned)
1 cup (¼ lb.) crumbled
  Roquefort or Blue cheese

dash pepper
¼ cup consommé or stock
  made with bouillon cubes
2 tbs. bread crumbs
butter

Arrange lima beans in layers in buttered baking dish. Sprinkle the crumbled cheese on each layer. Sprinkle each layer with pepper. The last layer should be lima beans. Pour consommé over limas. Sprinkle with bread crumbs and pepper. Dot with butter. Bake in moderate oven until top is crisp. Serves 4.

Variation Arrange alternate layers of cooked limas and Easy Cheese Sauce in buttered baking dish. Bake in moderate oven until top is golden and crisp.

MUSHROOM SURPRISE

½ lb. boiled ham, sliced
  thin
½ lb. mushrooms
½ tsp. salt
dash pepper

2 tbs. butter
½ lb. Swiss, Munster, Gold-
  N-Rich or similar cheese,
  sliced thin

Place slices of ham in buttered baking dish. Wash mushrooms and cut quickly into thin slices. Place over ham. Season mushrooms and dot with butter. Arrange slices of cheese over mushrooms. Bake in hot oven or under broiler until cheese is melted. Serve 3.

MUSHROOMS BAKED IN CHEESE SAUCE

1 lb. mushrooms　　　　　*2 cups Cheese Sauce or*
2 tbs. butter　　　　　　　*Mornay Sauce*
salt　　　　　　　　　　　*toast or hot rice*
pepper

The mushrooms for this dish should be on the small side. Wash them, remove stems and save for soup. If mushrooms are large, halve or, if necessary, quarter them. Place in buttered baking dish. Season and pour sauce over. Bake in moderate oven 20 to 25 minutes, or until nicely brown. Serve on toast or on fluffy rice. Serves 4.

BROILED MUSHROOMS WITH CHEESE

4 medium or large mush-　　*salt*
*　rooms per serving*　　　　*dash pepper*
½ tsp. butter per mushroom　*melted butter*
1½ tsp. grated Swiss or
*　Parmesan cheese per*
*　mushroom*

Wash mushrooms and remove stems. Place caps round side down in a buttered shallow baking dish. Mix butter and cheese into a paste. Fill each mushroom cavity with this paste. Season. Brush mushrooms lightly with melted butter, or dot with butter. Broil under medium heat for 5 to 10 minutes, depending on the size of the mushrooms. Serve on toast or fluffy boiled rice. Makes 1 serving.

BAKED ONIONS WITH CHEESE

8 medium-sized onions, boiled whole	a little top milk or cream to moisten
6 tbs. grated sharp Cheddar —it must be sharp	salt
2 tbs. bread crumbs	pepper
	butter

Scoop out onions, taking care not to damage shell. Mash onion insides fine. Mix with grated cheese and bread crumbs. Moisten with milk or cream, season, and mix until smooth. Stuff onions with mixture. Dot with butter. Bake in moderate oven until golden. Serves 4 to 8 people.

Variation   Beets may be used in the same manner as above.

ONIONS MENAGÈRE   The French eat lots of onions as a vegetable, and this is one of their fine ways of preparing them.

1 lb. onions	½ cup grated cheese
2 cups Easy Cheese Sauce	butter

Parboil onions. Arrange in buttered shallow baking dish. Pour sauce over. Sprinkle with grated cheese. Dot with butter. Broil until heated through and golden. Makes 4 servings.

Variation   Beets may be used in the same way as above.

CHEESE AND ONION PIE   One of my—and my family's—favorites for lunch or supper, with a green salad. It was dreamed up by the Borden Company, parents of Elsie the Cow and Elmer, and granddaddies of Beulah and Beauregard. No wonder it's good for old and young!

1½ cups fine soda cracker crumbs
½ cup butter, melted
2½ cups onions, sliced thin
2 tbs. butter
1½ cups milk, scalded
2 eggs
1 tsp. salt
¼ tsp. pepper
½ lb. package Borden's Chateau cheese, finely shredded

Combine cracker crumbs and butter and blend well. Press evenly in a deep 8-inch buttered pie plate. Fry onions in butter until slightly brown. Place on crumb crust. Scald milk; add to eggs slowly, stirring constantly. Add salt, pepper, and Chateau cheese. Pour over onions. Bake in a slow oven until a sharp knife inserted in the center comes out clean, or about 40 to 45 minutes. Serves 4.

PEASANT BREAKFAST A fine, hearty dish, good for a strong man's breakfast, or ordinary folks' luncheon or supper.

4 slices bacon
3 boiled potatoes, cubed
1 tbs. onion, finely chopped
½ tsp. salt
dash pepper
½ cup grated Cheddar cheese
5 eggs

Cut bacon into small pieces. Fry over low heat until slightly brown and crisp. Drain off all but 2 tablespoons of fat. Add potatoes, onion, and seasonings. Cook until potatoes are slightly brown. Sprinkle cheese over potatoes. Break eggs into pan over potatoes and cook over low heat, stirring constantly, until eggs are set. *Do not beat eggs beforehand.* Makes 4 servings.

COTTAGE CHEESE POTATO PIE A very pleasant and different way of using two of nature's healthiest foods, potatoes and cottage cheese.

½ recipe pie pastry

2 cups mashed potatoes, hot and seasoned

2 cups (1 lb.) cottage cheese

½ cup sour cream

2 tbs. onion, finely diced

1 tsp. salt

dash pepper

milk

1 tbs. butter

Line 9-inch piepan with pastry. Chill. Mix potatoes, cheese, cream, onion, and seasonings. Pour into pie shell. Brush top with milk and dot with butter. Bake in hot oven for 15 minutes. Reduce heat to moderate and bake 15 minutes longer, or until top is brown. Serves 4 to 8.

COTTAGE CHEESE POTATOES   A dish from Austria, where they eat lots of cottage cheese with potatoes, noodles, and just by itself.

2 cups diced, cooked potatoes

½ cup cottage cheese

4 slices crisp cooked bacon, crumbled

1 tbs. fine dry bread crumbs

Arrange alternate layers of potatoes, cheese, and bacon in shallow buttered baking dish. Sprinkle with bread crumbs. Place on lowest shelf of broiler and broil until slightly brown on top. Makes 4 servings.

Variation   The above ingredients may also be mixed in saucepan and heated over low fire.

POTATOES AU GRATIN

2 cups finely diced boiled potatoes

½ cup grated Cheddar cheese

1 tbs. finely diced onion
butter

1 egg

½ cup milk

1 tsp. salt

dash pepper

additional grated cheese

Arrange alternate layers of potatoes and cheese in buttered 1-quart baking dish. Sprinkle each layer with onion and dot with butter. Mix egg, milk, and seasonings. Pour over potato mixture. Sprinkle with additional grated cheese. Bake in moderate oven 25 minutes, or until set. Serves 4.

CHEESE POTATO CROQUETTES

6 large boiled potatoes,
  mashed hot
2 eggs
½ cup grated Cheddar or
  Swiss cheese
1 tsp. salt
¼ tsp. pepper
milk
bread crumbs
fat

Mix potatoes, eggs, cheese, and seasonings. Form into balls. Dip in milk and bread crumbs. Sauté in hot fat until brown on all sides.

These croquettes taste much better if a cube of cheese is put in the center of each. Make sure that cheese is completely covered, or else it will seep out. Serves 4.

CHEESE POTATO PUFFS

6 medium-sized potatoes
4 tbs. butter
½ cup hot light cream or
  top milk
2 eggs, separated
1 cup (¼ lb.) grated Cheddar cheese
melted butter

Peel potatoes. Cook in boiling salted water. Drain and shake over heat until dry. Mash well until free from lumps. Beat in butter and cream. Beat until fluffy. Add well-beaten egg yolks and cheese. Mix well. Fold in stiffly beaten egg whites. Place mounds of potatoes on greased baking sheet. Brush with melted butter. Bake in moderate oven 15 to 20 minutes, or until slightly brown. Makes 4 to 6 servings.

This mixture may also be heaped in a greased baking dish and baked in a moderate oven until puffy and brown on top.

STUFFED POTATOES DE LUXE

4 large baked potatoes
1 (3-oz.) can deviled ham
1 egg
1 cup (¼ lb.) grated Cheddar or Swiss cheese

½ tsp. salt
dash pepper
4 to 6 tbs. light cream or top
   milk
melted butter

Bake potatoes as usual. Cut in half and carefully scoop out potato, leaving skin whole. Mix with ham, egg, cheese, salt, and pepper. Gradually beat in cream or top milk until light and fluffy. Pile mixture into skins, brush with melted butter, and bake in hot oven 15 minutes, or until tops are slightly brown. Makes 4 to 8 servings.

SPINACH À L'ITALIENNE

2 lbs. spinach, cooked and
   seasoned
¼ cup olive oil—it must be
   hot

1 cup (¼ lb.) grated Par-
   mesan cheese
dash nutmeg

Arrange alternate layers of spinach, olive oil, and cheese in buttered baking dish. Add nutmeg. Bake in moderate oven about 15 minutes, or until brown on top.

This is a very good dish, but *the spinach and olive oil must be really hot* before being put in baking dish. Serves 4.

BAKED STUFFED TOMATOES

4 medium-sized tomatoes
salt
¼ lb. (1 cup) grated sharp
   Cheddar cheese
1 egg

4 tbs. heavy cream
1 tsp. chopped parsley
½ tsp. salt
dash pepper
bread crumbs

Wash tomatoes, cut slice off top and scoop out centers, taking care to leave tomato cup whole. Sprinkle lightly with salt. Invert to drain. Mix cheese, egg, cream, parsley, salt, and pepper. Fill the tomatoes. Sprinkle top with crumbs. Place in buttered individual baking dishes or buttered shallow baking dish. Bake in moderate oven 15 to 20 minutes until brown on top. Makes 4 servings.

Since the filling is quite thin, it's a good thing to serve toast fingers with this dish for dunking.

BAKED STRING BEANS WITH CHEESE   Home canners know that however they plan they always end up with a lot of string beans that must be eaten up before the next canning season comes around. This is a good way of making them more interesting.

2 cups (1 No. 2 can) cooked or canned string beans
¾ cup grated Cheddar cheese

½ cup light cream or top milk
½ tsp. salt
dash pepper
2 tbs. butter

Place beans in buttered baking dish. Mix remaining ingredients except the butter. Pour over beans. Dot with butter. Bake in moderate oven until beans are heated through. Serves 4.

ZUCCHINI SQUASH WITH CHEESE   A nice, though rather flat, vegetable made interesting.

1 medium onion, chopped
1 green pepper, diced
4 tbs. butter or cooking fat or oil
1 lb. zucchini squash, thinly sliced
1 tsp. salt
dash pepper
1 tsp. Worcestershire Sauce (optional)

2 (8-oz.) cans prepared tomato sauce
2 cups water
1 cup (¼ lb.) grated Tillemook or other Cheddar cheese
hot rice

Lightly brown onion and green pepper in butter or other fat. Add zucchini squash, seasonings, sauce, and water. Cover. Simmer until squash is tender, or about 15 minutes. Stir in cheese. Cook until melted. Serve on fluffy boiled rice. Makes 4 to 6 servings.

Variation Eggplant or other summer squash may be used in place of zucchini.

Fritters, Patties, Puffs, Hot Sandwiches, & Pancakes

PIZZA ALLA NAPOLETANA   The hearty, tasty Italian dish Americans love best after spaghetti, to judge from the number of shops where it's sold.

The real pizza (which means pie) is made with bread-dough. However, it also tastes good if made with biscuit dough from a biscuit mix. In this case, be sure to spread the dough very thin on the pie plate, because it rises consider· ably in cooking and spills the contents.

Line a 9-inch pie plate either with bread dough or biscuit dough. Brush dough generously with olive oil. Cover thickly with sliced Mozzarella or Jack cheese. As a reasonably satisfactory substitute you can use a very new Cheddar, or a semihard cheese, such as Munster—but try to get Mozzarella at your A & P or in a grocery in an Italian neighborhood. Cover Mozzarella cheese with tomatoes that have been cut in small pieces, or very well-drained canned tomatoes. Sprinkle with salt, pepper, ½ tablespoon grated onion (optional), and orégano (optional, too, but good). Brush with more olive oil. Cut a dozen anchovy fillets into small pieces. Place on tomatoes. Bake in a hot oven for 20 to 30 minutes. This is 1 serving.

If any pizzeria or pizza shop tries to sell you Pizza Alla Napoletana without anchovies, send it back and be forceful about it. The anchovies *belong* on it.

SPIEDINO ALLA ROMANA   This is one of the best Italian dishes, and also one of the simplest to make. The success depends on the cheese used, which must be Mozzarella or very new Monterey Jack. The A & P stores carry Mozzarella, as well as any groceries in an Italian neighborhood. Monterey Jack is a California cheese.

Remove the crust from a loaf of French bread. Cut loaf into slices about ⅓ inch thick. Cut cheese in the same size and thickness as bread. Place alternate slices of bread and cheese on a skewer until there are 3 of each—bread on the outside at each end—this is one helping. Preheat baking dish and place skewers in it. Bake in a very hot oven just long enough for the cheese to melt and the bread to brown. If the bread hasn't browned, place under broiler for a few minutes. Now prepare this *essential* sauce: Melt ½ pound butter. Chop 6 anchovy fillets and simmer in butter for 5 minutes. When bread and cheese skewers are done, pour sauce over each helping. Serve as hot as you can.

CHEESE KABOBS

6 1-oz. portions of Gruyère	*1 egg yolk*
cheese	*½ tsp. salt*
4 slices bread	*flour*
½ cup milk	*fat for deep frying*

Cut each portion of Gruyère in half. Cut each slice of bread into 4 triangles. Place alternate slices of bread and cheese on skewers, using 4 triangles of bread and 3 triangles of cheese. Mix milk, egg yolk, and salt. Dip each skewer into mixture and then sprinkle liberally with flour. Shake off excess flour. Fry each skewer in hot fat (365° F.) to cover for 2 to 3 minutes, or until lightly browned. Drain. Serve plain or with chili sauce or catsup. Makes 4 servings.

FRIED CHEESE   Very, very good.

8 slices Tilsit, Gold-N-Rich,   *1 tsp. salt*
  Gruyère, or any other   *⅛ tsp. pepper*
  semihard cheese   *1 cup fine dry bread crumbs*
1 egg   *butter*
½ cup milk

Remove rind from cheese. Cut into ⅛-inch slices. Mix egg, milk, and seasonings. Dip cheese in egg mixture, then dip in dry bread crumbs. Dip again in egg and crumbs. Fry in butter until browned on both sides. Serve hot. Makes 4 servings.

The slices may be dipped in egg and crumbs only once if desired, but the cheese is harder to turn and oozes out before it is completely browned.

CHEESE FRITTERS   All these cheese fritters, dumplings, puffs, et cetera, make very good-tasting, nourishing, and inexpensive main dishes.

1 cup flour   *½ tsp. finely chopped*
1 cup (¼ lb.) grated sharp   *parsley (optional)*
  cheese   *1 egg, separated*
½ tsp. salt   *2 tbs. melted butter*
dash pepper   *½ cup lukewarm water*
½ tsp. dry mustard   *fat for deep frying*

Sift flour. Add cheese and seasonings. Mix well. Combine well-beaten egg yolk, butter, and water. Add to cheese and flour mixture. Beat egg white until stiff but not dry. Fold into mixture. Carefully drop by tablespoons into deep, hot fat (365° F.). Fry until browned. Makes 8 fritters. Serve hot with tomato or chili sauce, or with catsup.

SWISS CORN MEAL OR FARINA CHEESE FRITTERS

¾ cup corn meal or farina
1 tsp. salt
3 cups boiling water
thin slices of your favorite
cheese

1 egg
breadcrumbs
butter or shortening

Cook cereal in boiling salted water, stirring constantly, for 5 minutes. Place over boiling water, cover, and cook about 45 minutes longer, or until water is absorbed. Stir occasionally. Pour on greased shallow pan or baking sheet about ¼. inch thick. Chill. Cut into squares or rounds to make pairs. Place cheese on half the fritters. Cover with remaining fritters. Dip in egg and bread crumbs. Fry in deep, hot fat (365° F.) until golden brown. Serves 4.

CHEESE PUFFS   A cheese-choux paste dish, which is especially suited for luncheons and suppers.

1 cup water
¼ cup butter
1 cup sifted flour
3 eggs

¼ cup grated Parmesan
  cheese
½ tsp. salt
dash of pepper

Put water and butter on heat. Bring to boil. Remove from heat. Add flour all at once. Beat until glossy and dough comes off sides of pan in a ball. Beat in eggs one at a time. Add cheese, salt, and pepper. Shape with pastry bag or with spoon on ungreased baking sheet. Place puffs about 2 inches apart to allow room for spreading. Bake in a very hot oven for 15 minutes, then reduce heat to moderate and bake 20 to 25 minutes longer. Cut slit in side of puff and fill with Mornay Sauce or Cheese Sauce, creamed chicken, creamed eggs, et cetera. Yield depends on size of puffs. Makes 4 to 6 servings.

CHEESE AND ANCHOVY AIGRETTES   A very French fritter, nice and tasty.

1 doz. fillets of anchovy   *fritter batter*
2 tbs. Thick Mornay Sauce   *fat for deep frying*
2 tbs. grated Swiss or
*   Parmesan cheese*

Cut fillets of anchovy into small pieces. Mix pieces with Thick Mornay Sauce. Add cheese. Drop spoonfuls of this mixture into fritter batter. Fry in hot fat, as with fritters. Serve sprinkled with some more grated cheese. Serves 4.

CHEESE BEIGNETS   Cheese Beignets are made from choux paste which is not sweetened, but flavored with cheese. They're excellent with drinks, tomato juice, or salads.

½ cup water   *1 tsp. salt*
3 tbs. butter   *dash pepper*
½ cup flour   *1 egg white, stiffly beaten*
2 eggs   *fat for deep frying*
4 tbs. grated Parmesan or
*   sharp Cheddar—the*
*   cheese must be sharp*

Put water and butter on heat. Bring to boil. Remove from heat. Add flour all at once. Beat until glossy and dough comes off sides of pan in a ball. Beat in eggs, one at a time. Add cheese, salt, and pepper. Fold in egg white. Drop from teaspoon into hot, deep fat (365° F.). Brown on all sides. Remove from fat and drain. Serve hot with additional cheese if desired. Beignets should be puffy and crisp. Makes about 3 dozen.

Variation   For an elegant main dish try this. Follow recipe above. Here is the change: drop by teaspoonfuls into boiling, salted water. Do not cover. Cook for about 5 minutes. Remove from water with a slotted spoon. Place on hot platter. Serve with brown butter and additional cheese. This is a feather-light dumpling.

CHEESE PATTIES

½ lb. (2 cups) your favorite process cheese, grated
1⅔ cups cracker crumbs **or** *1 cup fine dry bread crumbs*
4 tbs. butter, softened

1 tbs. finely chopped parsley or chives
2 tsp. prepared mustard
1 tsp. salt
¼ tsp. pepper
2 eggs, well beaten

Mix together cheese, crumbs, butter, parsley or chives, mustard, salt, pepper, and eggs. Shape into patties. Sauté over low heat until lightly browned on both sides. Serve hot with horse-radish, Creole, chili sauce, or catsup. Serves 4.

QUICK CHEESE PATTIES

4 to 6 patty shells made of puff pastry (may be purchased in bakery)
½ lb. (2 cups) Swiss grated
1 tbs. flour

½ tsp. salt
dash pepper
1 egg, slightly beaten
¾ cup sour cream

Mix cheese, flour, salt, and pepper. Add egg and sour cream. Mix well. Pour into patty shell. Bake in hot oven 20 to 25 minutes, or until set. Makes 4 to 6 servings.

SAVORY CHEESE SURPRISE

*1½ cups minced cooked
   corned beef or corned-
   beef hash
3 tbs. mustard
1 tbs. prepared horse-radish*

*6 slices bread
6 slices Tilsit, Munster,
   Brick, Swiss, or similar
   cheese*

Combine corned beef, mustard, and horse-radish. Spread on slices of bread. Cover with slices of cheese. Place in hot oven about 10 minutes until cheese is melted and golden brown. Serve at once. Serves 6.

SUPPER SNACKS

*4 slices bread
prepared mustard
8 stuffed olives, sliced
4 slices boiled ham*

*24 asparagus tips, cooked
4 ⅛-inch slices Cheddar or
   Swiss cheese*

Toast bread on one side. Spread untoasted side with mustard and sliced olives. Place ham on olives. Arrange asparagus tips on ham. Cover with slices of cheese. Place under broiler until delicately brown. Serves 4.

BLUE CHEESE OR ROQUEFORT SANDWICHES

*4 slices hot toast
butter
4 thickish slices Blue cheese
   or Roquefort cheese*

*chopped salted nuts or
   almonds*

Spread toast with butter. Cover with slices of cheese. Place in moderate oven 5 to 6 minutes. Sprinkle with nuts. Serve with salad. Makes 4 servings.

BAKED SANDWICHES DE LUXE

8 slices day-old bread
1 8-ounce can or jar deviled ham, tongue, or meat spread
8 slices Swiss or Cheddar cheese

1 egg, well beaten
¼ cup milk
½ tsp. salt
½ tsp. Worcestershire Sauce (optional)
dash pepper

Spread bread with meat. Place slice of cheese on each of 4 slices of bread. Put together sandwich fashion. Mix egg, milk, and seasonings. Carefully dip both sides of sandwiches in egg and milk mixture. Place on well-greased baking sheet or shallow baking dish. Top each sandwich with a slice of cheese. Bake in moderate oven 20 to 25 minutes, until cheese is melted and bread is lightly toasted. Makes 4 servings.

CHEESE SIZZLERS

4 English muffins or hamburger buns, split and toasted
1 3- or 4-ounce can deviled ham
¾ cup finely chopped onion

1½ tbs. butter
dash thyme
½ lb. process cheese, cut into 16 slices
4 tbs. catsup

Spread deviled ham on toasted muffins or buns. Cook onion in butter until soft and only lightly browned. Add thyme. Mix well. Spread over ham. Top each muffin or bun with 2 slices of cheese and catsup. Place under moderate broiler and broil until cheese is melted and lightly browned. Makes 4 servings.

CROQUE MONSIEUR A noble sandwich, one of the best ever invented.

8 slices stale bread	*8 thin slices Swiss cheese*
butter, softened	*1 cup Medium White Sauce*
4 slices boiled ham	*½ cup grated Swiss cheese*

Spread bread with butter. Then make into 4 sandwiches, using 2 slices of cheese and 1 slice of ham for each sandwich. Cut in half, and tie lightly with string. Sauté in melted butter until browned on both sides. Season white sauce with cheese. Heat until cheese is melted. Remove strings from sandwiches. Place 2 sandwiches on a plate, cover with sauce. Sprinkle with paprika. Makes 4 servings.

BAKED SANDWICHES, OPEN-FACE STYLE

4 tbs. butter	*1 cup (¼ lb.) diced Ched-*
4 tbs. flour	*dar or Swiss cheese*
1 tsp. salt	*1 egg yolk*
½ tsp. pepper	*4 to 6 slices day-old bread*
½ tsp. prepared horse-radish	*white wine*
1 cup milk	

Melt butter. Remove from heat. Blend in flour, salt, pepper, and horse-radish. Add milk, gradually mixing until well blended. Cook over low heat, stirring constantly, until thick and smooth. Remove from heat. Add cheese and egg. Mix until well blended. Dip bread in wine. Spread with cheese mixture. Place on greased baking sheet and bake in hot oven for 8 to 10 minutes, or until brown on top. Makes 4 to 6 servings.

Variations **1.** Top with sliced tomatoes before baking.

2. Mix ½ cup sliced sautéed mushrooms with cheese mixture.

3. Top with half-cooked bacon before baking.

SAUTÉED SANDWICHES SWISS STYLE

8 slices rye bread   8 slices Swiss cheese
butter   sliced tomatoes
prepared mustard

Spread bread with butter and mustard. Put 2 slices of cheese on each of 4 pieces of bread. Cover with second slice. Sauté in butter until brown on one side. Turn and brown on other side. Serve with cold sliced tomatoes. Makes 4 servings.

You can also use deviled ham in place of cheese.

PANCAKES WITH CHEESE   Use your favorite batter, but keep it on the thin side. For each 2-cup flour batch of batter add 1 cup of grated sharp cheese, such as Cheddar or Parmesan.

Pancakes Patron   Make cheese pancakes about 4 inches in diameter. Cook as usual. Remove from pan, keep warm. Spread each pancake with 1 tablespoon Cheese Sauce, or Thick Mornay Sauce (see pages 143, 144). Roll. Place in buttered shallow baking dish. Pour over additional sauce— if you have been using Thick Mornay Sauce, thin it a little. Bake or broil until brown and bubbly.

Pancakes with Mushrooms   Make Pancakes Patron. Substitute 1 tablespoon minced sautéed mushroom for cheese sauce filling. Proceed as above, covering with cheese sauce. Bake or broil until brown and bubbly.

Pancakes Julienne   Make slightly thicker cheese pancakes. Cut into strips about ½ inch wide. Roll in grated cheese. Place on buttered shallow baking dish. Cover with cheese sauce. Sprinkle with additional cheese. Place in oven or under broiler to brown.

NOTE: If you are planning to stuff your pancakes with cooked minced meats, add 1 cup of grated cheese per cup of meat.

COTTAGE CHEESE PANCAKES A nice nourishing dessert to top off a light meal.

1 cup flour
1 tsp. baking powder
1 tsp. salt
2 cups (1 lb.) cottage cheese
4 eggs, well beaten

4 tbs. top milk or light
  cream
butter
cinnamon and sugar

Mix together flour, baking powder, and salt. Add to cottage cheese. Mix until well blended. Beat eggs and milk or cream together. Add to cheese and flour mixture. Blend well. This should be the consistency of a medium pancake batter—it might be necessary to add slightly more cream or flour to achieve the right consistency. Fry in butter like any pancake. Serve with cinnamon and sugar. Makes about 8 pancakes.

DOUBLE-CRUST CHEESE PIE Good for picnics.

1 recipe pie pastry
1 lb. thinly sliced Cheddar
  or Swiss cheese

butter
cream

Line 8-inch piepan with pastry. Arrange slices of cheese on pastry. Dot with butter. Cover with top crust. Seal edges well. Make several slits on top. Brush top with cream. Bake in hot oven 20 to 25 minutes, or until pie is browned. Makes 4 to 6 servings.

Variations 1. Spread lower crust with deviled ham.
2. Sprinkle cheese layers with sliced sautéed mushrooms.

YORKSHIRE PUDDING WITH CHEESE In Yorkshire, the true pudding lovers are said to sit in the kitchen to wait till the pudding is ready. Then they sprint to the oven door and snatch the pudding, to eat it at the peak of perfection, when it is golden and puffy.

1 cup sifted flour
½ tsp. salt
½ cup grated Swiss or
  Cheddar cheese

2 eggs, well beaten
1 cup milk
butter

Sift flour. Sift again with salt. Stir in cheese and mix well. Beat together eggs and milk. Add to flour mixture and beat until smooth with rotary egg beater. Pour into a hot shallow baking dish generously greased with butter. Bake in hot oven 25 to 30 minutes. Cut into squares. Serve as usual. Serves 4.

Sauces

QUICK CHEESE SAUCE

½ lb. (2 cups) processed   ½ cup milk
American cheese, chopped
or grated

Melt cheese in top of double boiler over hot water. Add milk and stir until well blended.

This is a good sauce to *pour* over other foods. Makes about 2 cups of sauce.

WINE CHEESE SAUCE This sauce is good on vegetables, fish, and eggs.

½ lb. (2 cups) Swiss or any   ½ cup dry white wine
mild Cheddar cheese,   1 tsp. butter
chopped or grated

Melt butter in top of double boiler over hot water. Add cheese and stir until it is melted. Add wine, stirring constantly until well blended. Makes about 2 cups of sauce.

MORNAY SAUCE   Mornay sauce, like a soufflé, can be made with any kind of cheese. However, as in a soufflé, I think that a mixture of Parmesan and Swiss cheese gives the best flavor.

3 tbs. butter	*¾ cup light cream*
3 tbs. flour	*½ onion, if desired*
½ tsp. salt	*½ cup grated Parmesan*
⅛ tsp. white pepper	*cheese*
¾ cup chicken broth, home-	*½ cup grated Swiss cheese*
made or canned	

Melt butter. Remove from heat. Blend in flour and seasonings. Gradually add broth and cream, stirring until well mixed. Add onion, which must be in one piece. Cook over low heat, stirring constantly, until thick and smooth. Continue cooking 5 minutes longer. Remove onion. Add cheese and stir until well blended. This makes about 1½ to 2 cups of sauce, which may be used for fish, vegetables, eggs, etc.

SIMPLE MORNAY SAUCE

4 tbs. butter	*2 cups milk*
4 tbs. flour	*2 egg yolks*
1 tsp. salt	*1 cup (¼ lb.) grated Swiss*
¼ tsp. white pepper	*or other cheese*

Melt butter. Remove from heat. Blend in flour, salt, and pepper. Gradually add milk, stirring until smooth and well blended. Cook over low heat, stirring constantly, until thick. Beat in egg yolks and cheese. Cook 3 minutes longer. Makes about 2½ cups sauce.

VERY THICK MORNAY SAUCE   This thick Mornay Sauce is used for stuffing meats when a thinner one would run out.

½ cup butter
1 cup flour
1 tsp. salt
¼ tsp. pepper

1½ cups milk
1 cup (¼ lb.) grated Swiss
  cheese
2 egg yolks

Melt butter. Remove from heat. Blend in flour and seasonings. Gradually add milk, stirring until well blended. Cook over low heat, stirring constantly, until very thick and smooth. Stir in cheese and egg yolks. Cook until well blended and cheese is melted. Makes 2½ cups of sauce.

QUICK COTTAGE CHEESE DESSERT SAUCE

1 cup (8 ozs.) cottage
  cheese
⅓ cup heavy sweet or sour
  cream or evaporated milk

2 tbs. powdered sugar
½ tsp. vanilla

Beat cottage cheese, cream or milk, sugar, and vanilla until light and fluffy. Serve over fruit such as prunes, dried apricots, blackberries, et cetera. Makes about 2 cups of sauce.

EASY CHEESE SAUCE This sauce is good for au gratin dishes, baked cauliflower, baked macaroni or spaghetti, or whenever a cheese sauce is needed for cooking a dish.

3 tbs. butter
3 tbs. flour
¾ tsp. salt
½ tsp. Worcestershire Sauce
  (optional)

⅛ tsp. pepper
1½ cups milk
1 cup grated sharp Cheddar
  or Swiss cheese or 1 jar
  cheese with a smoky
  flavor

Melt butter. Remove from heat. Blend in flour and seasonings. Gradually add milk, stirring until well mixed. Cook over low heat, stirring constantly, until thick and smooth. Cook 5 minutes longer. Add cheese. Stir until well blended. This makes about 2 cups of sauce.

TOMATO CHEESE SAUCE This is a fine sauce for poached eggs, or poached or sautéed fish, baked spaghetti, noodles, and leftover meat casseroles.

3 tbs. butter	*2 cups tomato juice*
3 tbs. flour	*1 bouillon cube, broken into*
¾ tsp. salt	*pieces*
⅛ tsp. pepper	*1 cup (¼ lb.) grated sharp*
⅛ tsp. poultry seasoning	*Cheddar cheese*

Melt butter. Remove from heat. Blend in flour and seasonings. Gradually add tomato juice, stirring until well mixed. Add bouillon cube. Cook over low heat, stirring constantly, until thick and smooth. Cook 5 minutes longer. Add cheese. Stir until well blended. Makes about 2 cups of sauce.

Salads

CAMEMBERT MOUSSE

Good on a hot summer night with a vegetable or fruit salad. The Camembert must be very ripe. Get it a few days before it is to be used, and keep it at room temperature until it is quite soft.

6 ozs. Camembert
   (6 sections or a whole box)
1 tsp. prepared mustard
1 tsp. salt

dash pepper
1 cup heavy cream
1 egg white
lettuce

Pare the Camembert. Mash it until free of lumps. Blend in mustard, salt, and pepper. Beat cream until of custardlike consistency. Add to cheese. Fold in egg white that has been beaten until stiff but not dry. Pour into freezing tray of automatic refrigerator. Freeze until the consistency of soft ice cream. This may also be poured into a ring mold or any other fancy mold and frozen in the coldest part of the refrigerator or meat storage cabinet. Serve on lettuce. Makes 6 servings.

MOLDED CHEESE SALAD I

2 tbs. (2 envelopes) plain
  gelatin
¼ cup cold water
½ cup boiling water
2 (3-oz.) packages cream
  cheese
½ cup grated Cheddar
  cheese

⅓ cup Blue cheese
juice 1 lemon
⅛ tsp. pepper
1 tsp. salt
1 cup heavy cream, whipped
salad greens
lettuce and cucumbers

Sprinkle gelatin on cold water. Let stand 5 minutes and then dissolve in boiling water. Blend together the cream cheese, Cheddar, and Blue cheese until soft and creamy. Gradually beat in the lemon juice. Mix in salt and pepper. Stir in dissolved gelatin and mix until well blended. Fold in whipped cream. Pour into 8-inch ring mold which has been rinsed with cold water. Chill until firm. Unmold. Serve on crisp salad greens with sliced cucumbers and tomatoes. Makes 8 servings.

MOLDED CHEESE SALAD II

1 tbs. (1 envelope) gelatin
¼ cup cold water
½ cup boiling water
1 tsp. lemon juice
1 tsp. onion juice
1 tsp. dry mustard
1 tsp. curry powder
  (optional)

½ tsp. salt
1 cup (¼ lb.) grated sharp
  Cheddar cheese
1 cup (¼ lb.) grated
  Parmesan cheese
1 cup heavy cream, whipped

Sprinkle gelatin on cold water. Let stand 5 minutes and then dissolve in boiling water. Add seasonings and cheese. Stir until well blended. Fold in whipped cream. Pour into loaf pan (7½ × 3½ × 2 inches) or into individual molds which have been rinsed in cold water. Makes 4 to 6 individual molds, according to size.

FLORENCE'S COTTAGE RING MOLD

*1 tbs. (1 envelope) un-
flavored gelatin
¼ cup cold water
4 tbs. Blue cheese
1 cup (1 8-oz. package)
cottage cheese*

*½ tsp. salt
¼ tsp. paprika
½ cup heavy cream,
whipped
hot water
salad greens*

Soften gelatin in cold water. Dissolve over hot water. Cream Blue cheese. Blend in cottage cheese. Add seasonings and dissolved gelatin. Fold in whipped cream. Pour into 8-inch ring mold or 4 to 6 individual molds rinsed in cold water. This makes a ring mold that's about 1 inch thick. Unmold. Serve on crisp greens. Serves 4.

CHEESE AND HAM SALAD

*½ lb. boiled ham
3 hard-cooked eggs
1 stalk celery
½ lb. (2 cups) Cheddar
cheese*

*mayonnaise
lettuce
apples*

Put boiled ham, eggs, celery, and cheese through coarse food chopper. Add enough mayonnaise to moisten. Chill. Serve on lettuce with apple sections. Serves 6.

This salad may also be made by dicing ingredients and moistening with ½ cup French dressing.

CHEF'S SALAD   A famous salad that's easily made at home.

*4 cups assorted crisp salad
greens (lettuce, water
cress, endive, romaine, et
cetera)
¼ lb. Swiss cheese*

*1 cup boiled ham
1 cup cooked chicken
8 anchovies
salt and pepper
1 cup French dressing*

This salad should be mixed with the dressing just before serving or else it gets soggy. Place chilled salad greens in bowl. Sprinkle lightly with salt and pepper. Cut cheese into cubes. Cut ham and chicken into match-size pieces. Cut anchovies into small pieces. Mix greens, cheese, meat, anchovies, and seasonings. Let stand. Just before serving, pour over the dressing. Lightly toss to coat all ingredients well. Makes 4 servings.

SWEDISH LOBSTER SALAD

2 cups chilled cooked lobster　　mayonnaise
¼ lb. Gruyère, sliced　　capers
½ cup French dressing　　tomatoes
salad greens

Cut lobster into cubes. Slice cheese and mix with lobster and dressing. Mix well. Serve on crisp cold salad greens with mayonnaise, capers, and tomato slices. Makes 4 servings.

SIMPLE CHEESE SALAD

½ cup favorite French dressing　　¼ lb. (1 cup) Cheddar cheese, cubed
1 tsp. dry mustard　　1 tsp. chopped parsley (optional)
2 tbs. light cream　　lettuce or romaine
½ lb. (2 cups) Swiss cheese, cubed　　chopped parsley
　　paprika

Mix together French dressing, mustard, and cream. Pour over cheese. Let stand at room temperature for 1 hour, stirring occasionally. Just before serving, heap on crisp lettuce or romaine and sprinkle with parsley and paprika. Makes 4 servings.

PEPPER SALAD Stuff Simple Cheese Salad into green peppers which have been seeded and parboiled for 3 minutes. Chill. Garnish with sliced radishes.

TOMATO CUP SALAD Remove top from tomatoes. Scoop out pulp. Sprinkle lightly with salt and drain. Fill with Simple Cheese Salad. Chill. Garnish with sliced hard-cooked egg.

TOMATO AND CHEESE SALAD

4 tomatoes	*dash pepper*
½ lb. (2 cups) Swiss, Ched-	*dash nutmeg*
dar, or your favorite	*dash cayenne*
cheese	*½ cup salad dressing*
1 tbs. finely chopped onion	*lettuce and radishes*
½ tsp. salt	

Wash tomatoes and peel. Remove stem end. Cut into cubes. Cut cheese into cubes and mix with tomatoes and remaining ingredients. Chill. Serve on lettuce garnished with radishes. Serves 4.

COUNTRY SALAD   A hearty masculine salad.

4 cold boiled potatoes	*¾ cup mayonnaise*
½ lb. (2 cups) Swiss or	*½ tsp. dry mustard*
sharp Cheddar cheese	*½ tsp. Worcestershire Sauce*
1 cup diced celery	*lettuce and cucumbers*
¼ cup chopped walnuts or	
peanuts	

Cut potatoes and cheese into cubes. Mix with celery and nuts. Stir in mayonnaise, dry mustard, and Worcestershire Sauce. Let stand 1 hour in refrigerator. Serve on crisp lettuce garnished with cucumber slices. Makes 4 servings.

BRUSSELS SALAD   Like all cheese salads, a meal in itself.

4 Belgium endives	2 tbs. heavy cream
½ lb. (2 cups) Swiss cheese cut in fine cubes	juice 1 lemon
	water cress or lettuce
½ cup mayonnaise	stuffed olives
1 tsp. dry mustard	sliced tomatoes

Cut endives into slices. Cut cheese into cubes. Mix mayonnaise, mustard, cream, and lemon juice. Pour over endives and cheese. Mix lightly. Let stand ½ hour, stirring frequently. Serve on crisp water cress or lettuce garnished with sliced stuffed olives and sliced tomatoes. Serves 4.

MACARONI CHEESE VEGETABLE SALAD

¼ lb. elbow macaroni, cooked	2 tbs. diced green pepper
	1 tbs. minced onion
¾ cup cottage cheese	1 tsp. salt
½ cup cooked green peas	½ tsp. pepper
½ cup cooked diced carrots	⅓ cup salad dressing
¼ cup diced celery	salad greens

Combine cooked macaroni with other ingredients. Chill. Serve on crisp salad greens. Makes 4 to 6 servings.

COTTAGE CHEESE CUCUMBER SALAD

1 cup (½ lb.) cottage cheese	2 tbs. finely minced parsley
	½ tsp. salt
¼ cup sour cream	dash pepper
½ cup diced cucumber	salad greens
2 tbs. finely minced onion	ripe olives

Lightly mix all ingredients with fork. Chill. Serve on crisp salad greens, water cress, or escarole. Garnish, if desired, with ripe olive slices. Makes 4 servings.

FARMERS' SALAD

4 cold boiled potatoes
¼ lb. hard salami
½ lb. (2 cups) Swiss, Cheddar, or cheese food
1 large dill pickle

8 small picked onions
1 cup French dressing
lettuce
tomatoes
hard-cooked eggs

Slice potatoes and salami. Cut cheese into cubes. Chop dill pickle and onions. Mix all ingredients and marinate in French dressing in the refrigerator for 1 hour. Serve on lettuce garnished with tomato slices and hard-cooked eggs. Makes 4 servings.

FRENCH APPLE SALAD

4 red apples
2 tbs. lemon juice
1 cup diced celery
2 1-oz. packages Gruyère
cheese, sliced

½ tsp. salt
⅓ cup mayonnaise
lettuce

Wash apples, remove cores, and cut into pieces. *Do not peel.* Mix with lemon juice. Add celery, cheese, salt, and mayonnaise. Mix well. Lightly pile on crisp lettuce. Makes 4 servings.

STUFFED PEAR SALAD

8 halves canned or fresh
pears
⅔ cup (2 3-oz. packages)
cream cheese
3 tbs. Blue or Roquefort
cheese
2 tbs. cream

2 tbs. finely chopped olives
1 tbs. finely chopped onion
4 tbs. chopped salted al-
monds or other nuts
lettuce
fresh mint leaves

Drain pear halves if you are using canned pears. Blend ⅓ cup (1 3-ounce package) cream cheese, Blue cheese, cream, olives, and onion until smooth and creamy. Fill pears with mixture and put halves together. Chill. Just before serving, blend remaining package of cream cheese with 2 tablespoons pear syrup or cream. Lightly frost pears with mixture. Sprinkle with nuts. Place on crisp lettuce, and, if desired, put mint leaves at stem end of pear for garnish. Makes 4 servings.

SALAD ROLLS

*½ lb. (2 cups) your favorite
  cheese or cheese food,
  cubed
½ cucumber, cubed
½ cup flaked cooked tuna
  fish or chicken
⅓ cup diced celery*

*½ cup mayonnaise
8 small finger rolls
lettuce
tomatoes
green pepper rings
stuffed olives*

Mix cheese, cucumber, fish or chicken, and celery with ¼ cup mayonnaise. Slit rolls lengthwise, scoop out center. Stuff with salad mixture. Place on lettuce leaves. Surround with quartered or sliced tomatoes. Decorate top of salad rolls with mayonnaise, pepper rings, and thinly sliced stuffed olives. Serves 4 to 8.

BLUE CHEESE DRESSING   This dressing is especially suited to mixed salads.

*1 cup (¼ lb.) grated or
  crumbled Blue cheese
½ tsp. prepared mustard*

*¾ cup salad oil
3 tbs. vinegar or lemon juice*

Mash cheese and mix well with other ingredients. Shake before using. Makes 4 to 8 servings.

Puddings, Cakes, & Pastries

SWISS APPLE AND COTTAGE CHEESE PUFF A dessert the Swiss love. It's economical, nourishing, and good. The flavor depends on the tartness of the apples.

juice and grated rind of 1 lemon
1 lb. (4 or 5) apples, peeled and thinly sliced
1 cup (8 ozs.) cottage cheese
½ cup sugar

¼ cup farina or Cream of Wheat
2 tsp. baking powder
½ tsp. salt
½ tsp. grated nutmeg
3 eggs

Place juice and grated rind of lemon in mixing bowl. Slice in the apples, stirring occasionally, coating the apples with the lemon to keep them white. Blend in cottage cheese. Mix together dry ingredients and add to apple mixture. Add well-beaten egg yolks. Mix well. Fold in egg whites beaten until stiff but not dry. Pour into buttered 1½-quart baking dish. Bake in moderate oven 35 to 40 minutes, or until apples are tender. Serve with cream or fruit sauce. Makes 6 servings.

COTTAGE CHEESE DESSERT SOUFFLE This is a perfectly wonderful dessert, easy to make and sure to come out right.

2 tbs. butter
3 tbs. flour
½ tsp. salt
1 cup milk
3 eggs, separated
½ cup sugar
2 tsp. grated orange or lemon ring

½ cup toasted chopped almonds (optional)
½ cup raisins
1 cup (½ lb.) cottage cheese
bread crumbs

Melt butter. Remove from heat. Blend in flour and salt. Gradually add milk, mixture until well blended. Cook over low, heat, stirring constantly until thick and smooth. Beat egg yolks until light and lemon colored. Gradually beat in sugar and orange or lemon ring. Add almonds, raisins, cottage cheese, and White Sauce. Blend well. Beat egg whites until stiff but not dry. Fold into cheese mixture. Generously butter the bottom and sides of 1½-quart baking dish. Sprinkle thickly with fine dry bread crumbs. Carefully pour in cheese mixture. Place in shallow pan of hote water. Bake in moderate oven 50 to 60 minutes, or until top is brown and souffle is set. Serve warm from dish with fruit sauce. Makes 6 to 8 servings.

Variation 1 tablespoon rum may be substituted for the orange or lemon rind.

TURKISH CREAM CHEESE Turks like rich, sweet desserts, and that's the reason for the following dish. It's unexpected, and good.
    Break one 6-ounce package cream cheese into small pieces. Melt in saucepan over very low heat, stirring constantly. Serve hot with honey and squares of sponge cake. ladyfingers, or shortbread-type cookies. Makes 4 servings.

PASKHA The traditional Russian Easter dish—Paskha means Easter in Russian. It ought to be pressed in a tall wooden mold, bearing the sign of the cross, or the letters XB, the initials which mean "Christ is risen." Paskha is an excellent sweet, which deserves to be widely known among all the non-Russians.

¾ lb. (4 3-oz. cakes)
  cream cheese
½ cup sour cream
½ cup sugar
½ cup sweet butter
½ cup chopped blanched
  almonds

½ cup chopped orange and
  citron peel mixed
½ cup chopped seedless
  raisins

Mix all ingredients until well blended and smooth. Place in cloth or in mold that has been rinsed in cold water. Chill for 1 day. Unmold. Serve with plain cake. Serves 4.

CREAMED COTTAGE CHEESE PUDDING A refreshing dish, and a favorite of any children I've tried it on, including my own.

2 tbs. cornstarch
2 tbs. sugar
2 cups milk
2 eggs, well beaten
2 tbs. (2 envelopes) plain
  gelatin

3 tbs. sugar
1 cup (½ lb.) cottage
  cheese of the creamed
  variety
fresh or stewed fruit

Mix cornstarch and 2 tablespoons sugar in top of double boiler. Gradually add 1½ cups of the milk. Cook over boiling water, stirring constantly, until thick. Cover. Cook 15 minutes longer, stirring occasionally. Pour some of the hot liquid into eggs. Blend well. Pour back into hot sauce. Cook 3 minutes longer. Soften gelatin in remaining ½ cup milk. Add to hot sauce. Stir until gelatin is dissolved. Do not cook. Cool. Blend cottage cheese and the 3 tablespoons of sugar. Fold into cornstarch mixture. Pour into 8-inch ring mold. Chill. Unmold on serving dish. Fill center with fresh or stewed fruit. Makes 6 servings.

PETIT COEUR À LA CRÈME A favorite French dessert. Remember how pretty the Coeurs looked on their glistening grape leaves in the Paris markets?

Here are three versions which can be made in America. None of them tastes like true Coeur, but they come near it and are very good.

1

1 cup (8 ozs.) cottage cheese
1 3-oz. cream cheese
4 tbs. heavy cream
1 teaspoon rum, brandy, kirsch, or any non-sweet brandy (optional)

1 tbs. powdered sugar
dash salt

Blend cottage cheese with cream cheese. Gradually add cream, mixing until light and fluffy. Beat in sugar, salt, and brandy. Mold in heart-shaped little wicker basket that's typical of the dish by first putting damp cheesecloth into basket and then placing the cheese on the cloth. If you don't have any wicker baskets (fancy hardware stores carry them), any small individual dish will do. Serve with fresh strawberries, currant jelly, or any other fruit, or just with sugar and cream. Serves 4.

2

3 3-oz. packages cream cheese
4 tbs. heavy cream

1 tbs. powdered sugar
dash salt

Blend cream cheese and cream until soft and fluffy. Beat in sugar and salt. Chill. Serve with fresh fruit or with cream and sugar.

3

This is my favorite version of my favorite dessert. It's a little more acid than the others, and I think it comes closer to the original taste.

3 3-oz. packages cream
cheese
4 tbs. heavy sour cream
1 tbs. powdered sugar

dash salt
any non-sweet brandy
(optional)

Blend cream cheese and cream until soft and fluffy. Beat in sugar, salt, and brandy. Serve with fresh fruit or with cream and sugar.

GLORIFIED APPLESAUCE

1 cup (8 ozs.) cottage
cheese
3 tbs. sour cream
3 tbs. sugar

grated rind and juice of 1
lemon
½ cup thick applesauce
powdered nutmeg

Combine all ingredients but nutmeg. Blend well. Pour into serving dish. Sprinkle with nutmeg. Chill. Makes about 4 to 6 servings.

CHEESE DESSERT DUMPLINGS A dumpling that's popular in Austria and Czechoslovakia—a nice dessert after a light meal.

1 cup (½ lb.) cottage
  cheese
½ cup dry bread crumbs
½ cup sifted flour
2 tbs. sugar
½ tsp. salt

dash of nutmeg
2 eggs, well beaten
4 tbs. melted butter
boiling water
melted butter
powdered sugar

Mix cheese, crumbs, flour, sugar, salt, and nutmeg. Gradually add eggs and butter, mixing until smooth. Drop from tablespoon into boiling salted water. Cover. Cook 3 to 4 minutes. Remove from water with slotted spoon or large fork. Serve with melted butter and powdered sugar. Makes 12 to 18 dumplings, depending on size. Boiling fruit juice may be used in place of water for a tastier dumpling.

FRUIT CHEESE DESSERT DUMPLINGS   If you present your cheese dumplings in the following way to your Austrian friends, they will hug you and call you their very own.

Follow the recipe as for Cheese Dessert Dumplings, but before dropping into boiling water, roll dough into balls and put pitted cherry, prune, or apricot half in center. To roll dough successfully, flour hands well. Proceed as for Cheese Dessert Dumplings.

COTTAGE CHEESE DUMPLINGS

2 eggs
½ cup sour cream
1 cup (½ lb.) cottage
  cheese
¼ tsp. nutmeg

1 tsp. salt
2 tbs. sugar
1¼ cups sifted flour
hot water
salt

Beat eggs until foamy. Add cream and cheese. Mix well. Add nutmeg, salt, sugar, and flour. Mix well. Put ⅛ inch hot water in large shallow saucepan approximately 10 inches across and 3 inches deep. Salt lightly. Drop dumplings from teaspoon or tablespoon into water. Cover. Cook until water is evaporated. Take care not to burn in last minutes of cooking. Serve hot with jam, sugar, or fresh fruit sauce. Makes 8 to 16 dumplings, depending on size.

FRUIT-FILLED CHEESE TURNOVERS

¾ cup butter
1½ cups (¾ lb.) cottage cheese
2½ cups sifted flour
⅓ to ½ cup ice water
applesauce, apricots, peaches, jams, et cetera
milk

Cut butter and cottage cheese into flour with 2 knives or pastry blender. Gradually add water, mixing with a fork until just moistened. Wrap in waxed paper. Chill for 1 hour. Roll on lightly floured board and cut into circles or squares. Fill centers with applesauce, halves of apricots, sliced peaches, jam, dates, or raisins. Fold in half; pinch edges together with fork. Brush top with milk. Bake in hot oven 15 to 20 minutes. Makes 1½ dozen, depending on size.

CHEESECAKE

2 tbs. butter, softened
¾ cup zwieback or graham-cracker crumbs
½ cup sugar
2 cups (1 lb.) well-drained cottage cheese
⅔ cup (1 9-oz. can) crushed pineapple, well drained
¼ cup flour
1 cup heavy cream
3 tbs. lemon juice
1 tsp. grated lemon rind
½ tsp. vanilla
4 eggs, well beaten

Spread bottom and sides of 10-inch round cake pan with softened butter. Mix cracker crumbs and sugar. Sprinkle on pan, reserving 2 tablespoons for top. Combine remaining ingredients. Beat well. Pour into pan. Sprinkle top with remaining crumbs. Bake in slow oven 1 hour, or until a knife inserted in center comes out clean. Makes 8 servings.

MRS. HOPKINSON'S CHEESECAKE　A family recipe. Mrs. Hopkinson made her five daughters and their beaux happy with it.

2 cups graham cracker
　crumbs (22 crackers)
3 tbs. sugar
3 tbs. butter
½ cup cream cheese
　(1 8-oz. package)
¾ cup sugar

3 tbs. flour
1 tsp. grated orange rind
½ tsp. salt
½ tsp. mace
4 eggs, separated
½ pint (1 cup) heavy
　cream

Mix crumbs, the 3 tablespoons sugar, and butter. Press on bottom and sides of a well-greased 10-inch tube pan. Set aside. Cream the cream cheese until soft. Gradually beat in the ¾ cup sugar. Add flour, orange rind, salt, and mace. Stir in the well-beaten egg yolks. Blend well. Add cream and blend well. Fold in stiffly beaten egg whites. Pour into lined tube pan. Bake in slow oven 1 hour. Turn off heat. Let cake stand in oven until oven is cool. Carefully loosen sides and turn out on plate. Serves 8.

INEZ KUBLY'S SUPER DEVIL'S FOOD　This is *the* perfect chocolate cake. There is no more I can say—*the* perfect chocolate cake.

¾ cup cocoa (it must be
　cocoa)
1¾ cups sugar
4 eggs
½ cup sweet milk
½ cup butter
2 cups sifted flour

1 tsp. baking powder
1 tsp. baking soda
½ tsp. salt
1 cup sour cream
1 tsp. vanilla
Cream-cheese frosting

Cook cocoa, the ¾ cup sugar, 1 egg yolk, and sweet milk until thick. Stir constantly to prevent sticking. Cool. Cream butter until soft. Gradually add the remaining 1 cup of sugar, beating until well blended. Add 1 whole egg and 2 egg yolks. Mix well. Add flour sifted with baking powder, soda, and salt alternately with the sour cream. Add cocoa mixture, vanilla, and the 3 stiffly beaten egg whites. Pour into 3 waxed-paper-lined greased 8-inch layer pans or a 10-inch square pan. Bake in moderate oven about 30 to 35 minutes. Watch carefully. Do not overcook, because this cake must be moist. Use cream-cheese as frosting. Serves 6 to 8.

CREAM-CHEESE FROSTING

2 3-oz. packages cream	*2 tbs. confectioners' sugar*
cheese	*½ tsp. vanilla*
4 tbs. cream	

Soften cream cheese and mix with cream until fluffy and well blended. Beat in sugar and vanilla. The mixture may be used for toppings for any kind of cake or pudding.

BOHEMIAN CHEESE BUNS (KOLATCHEN)

1 recipe coffeecake dough	*1 egg*
(to serve 6)	*1 tbs. sugar*
1 tsp. powdered anise seed	*1 tbs. butter*
(optional)	*powdered nutmeg*
½ tsp. powdered cinnamon	*powdered ginger*
½ tsp. powdered mace	*salt*
⅔ cup cottage cheese	

To the coffeecake dough add the anise seed, cinnamon, and mace. Let rise until very light. Put on lightly floured board and roll out ½ inch thick. Cut into 3-inch rounds. Place rounds on well-greased baking sheet about 2 inches apart. Press in center with tablespoon to make a depression for the filling. Mix cottage cheese and remaining ingredients. Place on the dough. Cover the pan lightly and let the dough rise until double in bulk. Bake in moderate oven about 20 minutes, or until brown. Brush with browned butter and sprinkle with sugar. Makes 6 servings.

COTTAGE CHEESE DROP COOKIES

½ cup butter
¼ cup cottage cheese
1 tsp. vanilla
1 cup sugar

1 egg
2 cups sifted flour
½ tsp. soda
½ tsp. salt

Soften butter and blend with cottage cheese until creamy and fluffy. Add vanilla. Mix well. Gradually add sugar, beating until well blended. Add egg. Mix well. Stir in dry ingredients. Blend well. Drop from teaspoon onto greased baking sheet and bake in moderate oven for 10 to 12 minutes, or until delicately brown. Makes about 3 dozen cookies.

CREAM CHEESE FRITTERS   A highly original dish and an excellent one. But it's rich, so don't eat too much before you get to dessert.

1 egg, beaten
3½ tbs. flour
dash salt
*6 ½-inch slices cream
   cheese*

*any thick preserves or jam
   in which there are no
   pieces of fruit*
butter

Make thick batter with egg, flour, and salt. It might be necessary to add slightly more flour if egg is very large. Coat cream cheese with jam. Dip in batter, covering well. Sauté in butter until light brown on all sides. Serve with additional jam either hot or cold. Serves 4.

HUNTERS' SANDWICH DESSERT   There is no simpler dish—except that the ingredients must be really fresh and as good as can be.

Make a sandwich with *thin* slices of *fresh* white bread, using sweet butter (this is important) and cream cheese. Pour over it a generous amount of *real* maple syrup. It's delicious.

RUSSIAN CHEESE TARTS

1 recipe plain pie pastry
1 cup (½ lb.) cottage
 cheese
½ cup sour cream
2 tbs. sugar
½ tsp. salt

2 egg yolks
1 egg white
apricot or plum jam
 (optional)
milk

Line medium-size muffin pans with rounds of pastry, leaving overlapping edges. Mix cheese, cream, sugar, and salt. Beat egg yolks. Fold into cheese mixture. Beat egg white and fold into cheese mixture. If desired, place ½ teaspoon jam on bottom of each pastry-lined muffin pan, then add 1 tablespoon of the cheese mixture. Pinch edges of pastry together. Brush with milk. Bake in hot oven 10 minutes, reduce heat to moderate, and bake 20 minutes longer. Makes 12 to 14, depending on size.

COTTAGE CHEESE PASTRY   This is good pastry for tart or pie shells, turnovers, et cetera.

½ cup cottage cheese
¼ cup butter

½ cup sifted flour
½ tsp. salt

Mix cheese, butter, flour, and salt with pastry blender or 2 knives until well blended. Mix with a fork to form a ball of dough. Roll out thin on floured board. Cut into desired shapes. Fill with desired fillings, such as deviled ham, jam, fresh fruit, et cetera. Top with corresponding shape. Place on baking sheet and bake in hot oven 12 to 15 minutes, or until brown on top. Makes about 12 turnovers.

ABOUT CREAM CHEESE AND COTTAGE CHEESE

There are a great many other ways of using cream and cottage cheese besides spreading them on crackers, putting them in salads, and baking them into a cake. They are equally good and refreshing. I am especially fond of my cottage cheese recipes, because they ring changes in the use of cottage cheese, as nutritious and inexpensive a food as there ever was.

CHEESE DESSERT PIE

½ recipe pie pastry
1 cup (½ lb.) cottage
cheese
¾ cup sugar
2 tbs. flour
½ tsp. salt
grated rind and juice of
1 lemon

2 eggs, slightly beaten
1 cup milk
3 tbs. melted butter, cooled
½ tsp. vanilla
nutmeg (optional)

Line 9-inch piepan with pastry. Chill while making filling. Mix cheese, sugar, flour, and salt. Add lemon rind and juice. Combine eggs, milk, butter, and vanilla. Add to cottage-cheese mixture and mix until well blended. Pour into chilled pastry. Sprinkle with nutmeg. Bake in hot oven 10 minutes, then lower heat and bake 30 to 35 minutes longer, or until a knife inserted in center comes out clean. Makes 6 to 8 servings.

Sandwich Spreads, Brandied Cheeses, & How to Make Cheese

A VARIETY OF CHEESE SPREADS Any one of these spreads can be used in sandwiches, or for appetizers. Use dry toast, melba toast, or crisp crackers for the latter.

1. Mix 1 3-ounce package cream cheese, 4 tablespoons cream, ½ teaspoon salt, ¼ teaspoon paprika, and 4 tablespoons sherry wine until mixture is soft and smooth.

2. Cream 1 3-ounce cream cheese until soft. Add ½ teaspoon salt, ¼ teaspoon dry thyme, and ¼ teaspoon dry rosemary. Stand in refrigerator for 1 or 2 days, so that the cheese is well flavored.

3. Mix 3 ounces Limburger with ½ cup butter, 2 tablespoons grated onion, and ¼ teaspoon salt until smooth.

4. Cream 4 ounces Blue cheese with 2 tablespoons Thousand Island Dressing.

5. Any semihard cheese, such as Limburger, Camembert, Brick, et cetera, is good mashed and mixed with a generous sprinkling of crisp cooked and minced bacon.

6. Cream equal parts of Camembert and sweet butter. Shape into balls and serve with crisp crackers.

7. Grate Sap Sago. Used for grating, this very sharp, green, and herb-flavored cheese comes from Switzerland. Mix equal quantities of Sap Sago and butter and a sprinkling of caraway seeds until smooth. Spread on thin slices of dark bread. Or spread the above paste, omitting the caraway seeds, on bread. Top with ham or other cold cuts.

SANDWICH FILLINGS WITH PROCESS CHEESE OR WITH CHEESE FOOD

Allow ½ lb. package cheese to stand at room temperature until softened. Blend in *one* of the following ingredients:

1. *Two chopped hard-cooked eggs.*

2. *Four tablespoons minced green pepper.*

3. *Two-third cup finely chopped walnut meats.*

4. *Four tablespoons chopped nutmeats and 6 tablespoons finely chopped stuffed olives.*

5. *Three tablespoons butter and 4 tablespoons anchovy paste.*

6. *One-half cup finely chopped salted peanuts and ¼ cup finely chopped parsley.*

7. *Four tablespoons prepared horse-radish.*

ANCHOVY CHEESE SPREAD

1 (3-oz.) package cream cheese
2 tbs. cream
¼ tsp. salt

dash pepper
dash Worcestershire Sauce
2 tsp. anchovy paste

Have cheese at room temperature. Mix with remaining ingredients and blend well. Serve on melba toast, crisp crackers, or toasted rye bread.

MALAXÉ Malaxé means mixture, and this one comes from Normandy, where both the cheese and the hard cider are very, very good.

½ cup mashed Roquefort or   2 tbs. Calvados, Armagnac,
  Blue cheese   applejack, or brandy
½ cup butter

Mix cheese with butter until smooth. Add liquor. Mix until smooth and creamy. Spread on dry toast or on dark breads such as rye or pumpernickel.

SACHER CHEESE A spread invented by the famous Frau Sacher of Vienna, who entertained royalty in her restaurant, and invented the equally famous Sacher Torte.

½ lb. (1 cup) cottage cheese   3 anchovies
2 hard-cooked egg yolks   ¼ cup softened butter

Force cheese, egg yolks, and anchovies through a sieve. Beat together with butter until well blended. Chill. Serve on crisp crackers.

CRÈME DE CAMEMBERT A superb spread, as made by the great French-English cook and writer Marcel Boulestin.

Use a box of ripe Camembert for this. It must be really ripe, so keep it at room temperature until it is soft and runny. Place cheese in deep dish—you can peel it or not. Pour wine over, just to cover, no more, if anything, rather less. The wine should be a dry white wine of the Rhine, Riesling, or Chablis type. Steep cheese in wine for 12 hours. Take half as much butter as you have cheese. Work carefully into the Camembert until a smooth paste is achieved. Reshape into a round and serve with crackers as cocktail spread or dessert.

LIPTAUER SPREAD Liptauer is one of those things about which people from Central Europe have not only gastronomical affection, but also strong emotions. But, like Southerners and mint juleps, there are a lot of opinions what the real, the true Liptauer is like. This is an Austrian version—and may the Hungarians, Czechs, Bavarians, and other addicts forgive me. I may add that these are strong beer countries, and that Liptauer is wonderful with beer.

1 cup (8 ozs.) pot cheese
1 cup butter
1 anchovy
2 tsp. caraway seeds
2 tsp. capers

½ tsp. French mustard
½ tsp. salt
¼ tsp. white pepper
3 to 4 tbs. sour cream
paprika

Force pot cheese through sieve. Cream with butter until well blended. Add remaining ingredients, mixing well. Chill. Serve with rye bread, pumpernickel, or crisp crackers.

CHEESE SLIP

3 (3-oz.) packages cream cheese **or** *¾ lb. dry cottage cheese*
½ cup heavy sour cream
2 bouillon cubes

2 tbs. hot water
1 tbs. finely minced onion or chives
1 tbs. finely minced parsley

Soften cream or cottage cheese. Gradually blend in sour cream, beating until smooth and fluffy. Add bouillon cubes which have been dissolved in water, onion, and parsley. Mix well. Let stand several hours in refrigerator. Serve cold with potato chips, crisp crackers, or melba toast.

SIMPLE SANDWICH FILLING Cream together until soft and smooth 1 cup grated cheese (Swiss, Cheddar, cheese food, et cetera) and ½ cup butter. Spread on rye bread or spread on any other bread and place under broiler until slightly brown.

CHEESE TUNA SPREAD Blend together 1 cup grated Parmesan cheese and 1 cup flaked canned tuna fish. Spread on toast and serve with sliced tomatoes.

This mixture may also be spread on toast and placed in broiler until slightly brown. Makes enough spread for 6 to 8 sandwiches.

DUTCH CHEESE SPREAD

1 quart unpasteurized milk   *2 tbs. cream*
boiling water   *½ tsp. salt*
2 tbs. milk   *pepper*

Pour milk into earthen bowl. Stand in warm place to thicken. When quite thick, pour boiling water over it. Place in cheesecloth bag and drain 12 hours. Rub 1 cup cheese through a fine sieve. Soften by working in milk and cream. Season and eat on buttered bread.

SIMPLE BRANDIED CHEESE Combine ¼ pound (1 cup) crumbled Blue or other cheese with ¼ pound (½ cup) butter and 3 tablespoons brandy. Blend together until smooth. If the cheese is to be kept for any length of time, place it in a jar and cover with clarified butter or paraffin.

MRS. GLASSE'S POTTED CHESHIRE CHEESE I have tried this, and it's as good now as it was around 1770.

Take 3 pounds of Cheshire cheese (natural Cheddar) and put it into a mortar with a half pound of the best fresh butter you can get. Pound them together, and in the beating add a gill (¼ pint) of rich Canary wine, (Mrs. Glasse must have meant Madeira. I think brandy is better) and half an ounce of mace finely beat then sifted to a fine powder. When all is extremely well mixed, press it hard down into a gallipot, cover with clarified butter, and keep cool. A slice of this excels all the cream cheese that can be made.

HOW TO MAKE BRICKBAT CHEESE

HOW TO MAKE BRICKBAT CHEESE Mrs. Glasse was the most famous cookbook writer in the eighteenth century. Her *Art of Cookery Made Plain and Easy* (my edition says London, 1796, and it is one of the later ones) is a practical book from which I've cooked several very successful dishes. I haven't made Mrs. Glasse's cheese, but here it is.

Take 2 gallons of unpasteurized milk and a quart of good cream. Heat the cream, put in 2 spoonfuls of rennet, and when it is come (thickened), then put it in a wooden mold in the shape of a brick. It must be half a year old before you eat it. You must press it a little to help dry it.

KOCHKAESE OR BOILED CHEESE

KOCHKAESE OR BOILED CHEESE I consider Kochkaese an acquired taste. But lots of people have acquired it, and you may be one of them.

2 lbs. fine cottage cheese, about	1 tbs. flour
	½ cup milk
1 tsp. salt	pepper
2 tbs. caraway seeds	butter
2 egg yolks	

Rub cottage cheese through sieve. Place in earthenware or similar dish and set aside in the refrigerator for 1 week. Stir 2 or 3 times during the week. When the cheese has become quite strong, stir in salt, caraway seeds, and egg yolks. Mix milk and flour until smooth. Add about ½ to ¾ cup butter. Combine cheese and milk-flour-butter mixture. Bring to a boil and boil for about ½ hour, stirring constantly. The cheese must be very smooth. Pour into dish that has been rinsed in cold water. Store in cold place. If the cheese is not eaten immediately, cover it with a clean cloth that has been dampened with beer. Serve with rye bread and beer.

SOUR MILK COTTAGE CHEESE It isn't worth making your cottage cheese unless you have an ample supply of unpasteurized milk. However, if the spirit moves you, this is the way to do it, or, rather, one of the ways.

1 qt. sour or clabbered milk   *cream*
(skim, whole, or butter-   *salt*
milk)

Heat milk over hot water until lukewarm (95° F.) and it curdles and thickens. Remove from heat. Let stand in warm place for a few minutes for curd to collect. Turn into cheesecloth-lined strainer and let whey drain off thoroughly. If milk was very sour, rinse curd with cold water and drain again. Tie ends of cloth together and let hang until all the liquid has drained off. Moisten with cream or sour milk and season with salt.

Good with chives, onion, caraway seeds, olives, et cetera.

SWEET MILK COTTAGE CHEESE

1 rennet tablet   *2 tbs. cream*
1 pt. (2 cups) unpasteurized   *¼ tsp. salt*
milk

Crush rennet tablet to powder and dissolve in a tablespoon of the milk. Heat remaining milk until lukewarm. Test by putting a drop on your wrist. It must feel just warm. Stir in rennet. Stand in warm place until mixture thickens. Cut up thickened milk with knife into half-inch squares. This is done by running the knife through milk first in one direction and then the other. Place in cheesecloth bag. Hang bag with milk mixture so that it can drain thoroughly. After 2 or 3 hours remove mixture from cloth. Moisten with cream, season, and chill. Makes about ¾ cup of cheese.

Menus

In every household there is a time when you'll want to build up your meal around some entrée other than a meat dish. Don't throw up your hands in despair about what to do. Here are some suggestions for menus that will nourish your nearest and dearest—not to mention friends —in the proper way and make them come back for more and more.

Let's begin with lunch. The beauty of this menu is that it's as popular with mixed company as with the girls or your husband's business friends.

Chicken Hash Mornay (see page 96)
Tossed Green Salad or a Dish of
Water Cress Dressed with Olive Oil and Lemon
Lemon Meringue Pie

The wolf is at the door. You've got to save money, and you are stuck with a lot of last year's canned vegetables. Here's the way to be thrifty and to feed the folks what's good for them in a painless way.

Springtime Vegetable Pie (see page 117)
Coleslaw
Homemade Ice Cream and Cookies

Your husband has to have that big loan to enlarge his business. At the last country-club dance your local banker showed that he thinks you quite a little woman. It's obvious—you'll invite him to dinner and dazzle him with your cooking. But he is known as a *bon vivant* who's eaten in all the famous bistros. So you'll be different, and serve him a dinner with one perfectly prepared *pièce de résistance* we wager he doesn't know. Keep everything else very simple—the main dish will do the work for you.

Oysters on the Half Shell
(If they're not in season, have a cup of turtle soup laced with
good sherry—the imported medium dry kind.)
Fillet of Porterhouse à la Roquefort (see page 88)
A Salad of Unbroken Belgian Endives
(Separate the stems carefully and dress with a drop of olive
oil and lemon juice.)
Cherries Jubilee

Your old friend Joe Doakes is dropping in for an afternoon's chat. You haven't seen him for a long time. Not that there was ever a sentimental bond between you, but still you'll want to show him what he would have missed, had either you or he willed things differently.

Galettes (see page 68)
You make them as you go along talking, taking care they're
piping hot and as crisp as can be. The drink—give him his
choice of coffee or a good dry white or red wine.

It's Lent, and your favorite padre is coming to dinner. He's by no means unsophisticated, nor is the guest of honor, a famous lady novelist he's wanted to meet. Here's a suggestion for a dinner that will convince them that you've learned to combine the spiritual and the temporal in an admirable manner.

Grapefruit Broiled with Sherry and Brown Sugar
Coquilles St. Jacques (see page 85)
A Macedoine of Baby Vegetables
Cooked Separately in Sweet Butter and then combined.
(Of course they're served after the Coquilles)
Mousse au Chocolat

Another Sunday dinner *en famille,* you are thinking. Cousin Elmer and Aunt Rosa will be there, and everybody is expecting roast beef, of course, with all the fixings. Here's a nice change from the dreadful monotony of it all.

Celery-Stuffed cheese
Roast Beef with Yorkshire Pudding with Cheese
(see page 142)
Cauliflower Parmesan
Ice Cream and Cake

Uncle Ebenezer is coming to town on his yearly trip from Boston. You're fond of the old boy, and, besides, he has that silver teapot you've always felt should be your very own. Uncle Ebenezer loves to eat at all times. When he comes to the big city, however, he wants more—delicious food with a slightly sinful air, to remind him he's still naughty, still in the swim. Your problem is how to make him happy keeping his digestion unimpaired, so that he'll go back to Boston feeling gratefully young and gay.

A Cup of Clear, Hot Consommé with
Cheese Meltaways (see page 53)
Crème Lorraine (see page 76)
Buttered Baby Carrots
A Compote of Fresh Fruits Chilled in Kirsch

You're feeling rural, doing a Marie Antoinette all over the garden to dazzle your devoted guests. Supper is to be simple—everyone has had quite enough to drink and to nibble as is. What will restore the stomach, revive the spirit?

Henriette Seklemian's Excellent Leek Soup (see page 62)
Camembert Shortbread (see page 51) with a
Green Salad for those who have strength to eat it
Fresh Fruit

You like having your friends for Sunday brunch. In fact, you're famous for outdoing yourself on this most pleasant of all ways of spending a winter Sunday morning. Here's a new main dish, wonderfully staying when the wind blows cold and the snow is coating the windowpanes.

Fruit Juice in Large Pitchers
Peasant Breakfast (see page 125)
Stacks of Hot Buttered Toast with
Cooper's Oxford Marmalade
Coffee that's strong, hot, and served with hot milk for
them that wish it.

The children are tired of wholesome, bland, nondescript food. After all they are people, too, whatever grownups think. You see the justice of their laments, you decide to give them something quite different for a change, as wholesome as their usual diet, but much, much more interesting.

Sautéed Sandwiches Swiss Style (see page 140)
Zucchini Squash with Cheese
All the Ice Cream they can hold

Out shopping, whom should you meet but your beloved Estelle of boarding-school days? You haven't seen each other for donkey's years. With interest you note the fault-less tailleur, the sable stole, the made-to-order handbag, and calf pumps your once unprepossessing friend has de-veloped into. Of course you must have lunch and talk. Where? At my home, of course you say, already in a dither about what to serve to such a worldly creature.

Spiedino alla Romana (see page 132)
A Salad of Belgian Endives and Grapefruit Sections with
French Dressing
An Assortment of Perfect Fresh Fruits

Heaven knows why, but in a weak moment you've let yourself in for one of those bridge parties where your guests come to eat their dessert and coffee with you. Well, there it is—you've got to face it. So why not try something different on the eager girls—some dessert they're sure not to have had before?

Cottage Cheese Soufflé (see page 156) or
Mrs. Glasse's Potted Cheshire Cheese (see page 171)
with Plain Crisp Crackers
Coffee with Heavy Cream

The season is drawing to a close, and you have a guilty conscience about all the people who've invited you and whom you never invited back. You simply have to have a payoff, and in view of your neglect, it's got to be a real nice one. On the other hand, so you think, why not invite all the victims of your neglect for a real elegant buffet, so that they can entertain one another? Your main dish will be

Ham Hôtelière (see page 92)
Boiled Fluffy Rice
Spinach à l'Italienne (see page 128)
(Surrounded by all the fixings you consider
essential for a buffet)
Peach Melba in a Big Glass Bowl

Your son has announced his engagement to his darling from the Golden West. Her parents are hurrying East to see if he's really worthy of their treasure. That means you, of course—a thorough look over, down to the last inch of your furniture, to the last morsel of the introductory lunch. The problem is to prove that you are nice folks, with plenty of prestige that'll encourage the old man to part with a nice slice of his best stocks and securities.

> *Gnocchi alla Romana (see page 108) with*
> *Mushroom Surprise (see page 122)*
> *Tossed Green Salad*
> *Brandied Whole Peaches with Plain Heavy Cream*

A famous publisher is coming for dinner. Being a great man, he doesn't stoop to punctuality, though at least he has the decency to warn you beforehand. He has been everywhere, done everything—in fact he's his own walking monument. By chance you've discovered a penchant for Switzerland—we will not repeat the details given by your friends' evil tongues. This is the occasion for him to officiate at a

> *True Swiss Fondue (see page 72)*
> *followed by sinfully black and strong coffee and plenty of*
> *imported Swiss Kirsch*

Your brother-in-law, who lives in a twenty-four room apartment on Park Avenue and maintains a home at Southampton and Boca Grande as well, has once more irritated you with his favorite quotation: "We can live without friends, we can live without books, But civilized man cannot live without cooks," by whom he means the haughty Anatole he imported from Lyons. This time I'll show you, you think, and invite him to dine entirely on cheese dishes, to show that you, too, can be original. With imported very dry Sherry you serve

> *Raw Mushroom Canapés (see page 54)*
> *and small Cheese Beignets (see page 135)*
> *Veal à la Valdostana (see page 95) with*
> *Florentine Spinach*
> *Mrs. Hopkinson's Cheesecake (see page 162) or*
> *Petits Coeurs à la Crème with Bar le Duc*

These are but a few suggestions of the endless variety of menus with cheese. As I said before, cheese is as nourishing as meat, and very often a great deal nicer to eat. It's one of the substances men like, and I've tried to give you the kind of dishes that will win you mink coats rather than angry bellows from the man in your life. Go on and try for yourself your favorite combinations—it's easy and lots of fun!

Index